BURNED

Stop Getting Conned by Fake Coaches in the Personal Development Explosion

BY AARON NASH

Edited by Hilary Jastram, www.jhilcreative. com

DEDICATION

This book is dedicated to the Arete Syndicate.

Arete has truly changed my life and provided real, tactical business and leadership information that has made my businesses better.

More importantly, it has made me a better man.

Throughout this book, I will be discussing many topics, strategies, and personal experiences that lead me to find the truth. The Arete Syndicate is the greatest entrepreneurial and personal development group ever created.

To Ed Mylett and Andy Frisella, both dear friends, thank you for being the light in the darkness. Thank you for being the leaders of reality and truth. Thank you for changing my life.

This book is also dedicated to every fake influencer, scam, mastermind, guru, and "success" coach.

I am also dedicating my time and resources to exposing you. YOU are what is WRONG with this world. YOU are what has turned the personal development/entrepreneurial space into liars and thieves.

I dedicate this book to your downfall and to making you understand how detrimental your ego and carelessness are to every person looking for answers and guidance.

This book will give people the truth about not only what you do, but it will let them know how to audit you.

Everyone deserves the answers, for the curtain to be pulled back, and they deserve the truth. The truth is that you are not only uninformed, inexperienced, and unsuccessful, but that you prey on good people.

That can never be tolerated.

Our country, our businesses, and our families have been through too much to allow your lies anymore. My strongest dedication is for you to become an unemployed coach. I have all the faith that this will happen simply by you being who you are.

RESOURCES

Follow me on Instagram: @aaronnash20 and access your self-assessment coaching form.

Follow me on Facebook: Facebook.com/aarondnash

Live the Platinum Standard of Fitness: Pfitstudios.com

Health, fitness, and exercise coaching: Waytnutrition.com

Information on owning a P-Fit franchise: Pfitfranchise.com

TABLE OF CONTENTS

Foreword 4

Introduction 3

Chapter 1 – Read This Before You Hire a Coach 7

Chapter 2 – Don't Be Me 19

Chapter 3 – Questions to Ask Before you Give a Coach
    Any Money 25

Chapter 4 – Do You Even Need a Coach? 35

Chapter 5 – Acknowledging and Addressing Your
    Weaknesses 47

Chapter 6 – Defining Direction… and a Little Clarity 53

Chapter 7 – But I Like Them 63

Chapter 8 – Good Marketing Isn't Good Coaching 71

Chapter 9 – How to Tell Who is Full of Crap 75

Chapter 10 – Measuring ROI: What Are You Buying? 79

Chapter 11 – Have a Goal, Then Do Something with It! 87

Chapter 12 – You Don't Start at the Highest Level 99

Chapter 13 – Vet Your Network Like You Vet Your Coaches 105

About the Author 111

Disclaimer 113

FOREWORD

Contrary to what you may believe, no man or woman ever achieved anything great on their own.

Every person who ever reached a high level of success did so with the help of others. That's especially true today. The world moves faster than ever and is more competitive than ever. So it follows that the need for the right strategic alliances is more important than ever.

Aaron Nash wrote *Burned* for times like these.

I've known Aaron for many years. He's a hard charger. He's blunt and takes no prisoners. He is also successful. Very successful. But he will be the first to tell you he didn't get where he's at on his own.

He has a great team of employees, and they deserve tremendous credit. But throughout his entrepreneurial journey, Aaron has also sought out coaches and mentors who have helped his business leapfrog and grow exponentially.

Aaron was smart to connect with the right people to guide him.

It didn't happen by accident.

He was methodical and thought long and hard about what he needed. Early on, he understood that one wrong step or alliance can set you back for years, or completely torpedo your efforts.

Aaron discovered the multiplier effect of working with a good coach, some of it through trial and error, and some of it through his dogged trademark determination. He learned a lot along the way, and now he's ready to assume the mantle of leadership and help you reach your highest potential, too.

That's why he wrote *Burned.*

If you have even the smallest amount of ambition in your life, *Burned* is a must-read.

Let's be clear.

Finding and working with the right coach won't guarantee your success.

It's only the first step of many you'll need to take, but it can heavily increase your chances of reaching your goals.

Ultimately, it's up to you to put in the work and make things happen.

Ben Newman
Performance Coach
#1 *Wall Street Journal* and *USA Today* Bestseller,
Uncommon Leadership Podcast host, *The BURN*

INTRODUCTION

Allow me to disclaim this whole book upfront.

I am not a coach, and I didn't write this book to make money.

I wrote it to show you how to assess where you are so you can determine where you want to go.

To teach you how to audit, vet, and sniff out the bull of 99% of the coaches who fake it and offer no value.

To help you narrow down your list of remaining prospective coaches so that you can evaluate price, value, and utilize that information to explode your business and personal development exponentially.

When you finish reading, I want you to feel confident about choosing the right coach for you.

For now, keep going as I will cover the following topics and more to use when you are looking for a coach.

- Your responsibilities to your coach
- Your coach is not your buddy
- How do you choose a coach when it seems every person we meet is one these days?
- Coaches can sense your desperation

- Research before you hire
- No barrier to entry means you get all kinds of coaches
- Coaches should vet themselves
- Play by the coach's rules first
- Make the decision for you—not to fit in with other people flocking around a popular coach
- How to build credibility in your network
- Understanding what your dollars are buying
- Finding the courage to walk away after hiring a coach who is not right for you

I was a typical startup business owner just like you, and I still am. As an incredibly young man, I still have so much to learn.

But I want to teach you what I have learned to save you pain, grief, and money.

As I grew from being a small business owner, I became self-aware through reading, researching, and growing my business. I realized I needed to be around people, brands, and business owners who were going where I wanted to go.

This book explains how I did it, what I do every time I want to invest more into personal development, and how I have been burned yet can still win big while establishing the processes detailed in this book.

My goal is to help you. I don't sell anything in the book for a reason. I don't want this to be a pitch, a call-to-action, or a lead generator. I simply want you to learn about the mistakes I have made, that I see others make every day, and how to avoid them tactically as you progress through your journey.

This book is written so as you grow in your journey and re-read it, the information will be applicable at any time. It will be relevant for as long as the internet and social media exist, and even beyond. When you read it, you can save time—our most valuable asset. You'll also save yourself money and avoid the frustration and helplessness of going through the process of vetting a coach. You need to know this as people trying to be coaches are becoming more and more prevalent cancer in our society.

I've done the work to help you navigate how to find and hire a coach and identify what you need to know before taking the leap.

I've gotten my knuckles bloody and sat with my head in my hands late at night, wondering what the hell to do next. I've worried about how to pay my team and felt so alone in coaching and making all my decisions. Sometimes, I was unsure if what I chose to do in certain moments was the right thing. I've made more mistakes than I've had successes. I've wasted money on coaches. Maybe you have, too?

I don't want either of us to throw away another dollar on wanna-be coaches who can't do a damn thing for us.

We are too valuable, and our businesses and goals are too important to be treated so shallowly. After all, your business runs on your experience and the experience of the people you invest in to help you.

This book will teach you how to evaluate every coach, mastermind, personal guru, and networking group based on what you actually need. When you are done reading it, you will have the skills to hire any coach or join any mastermind or networking group on Earth.

Keep it close by for those moments when you know you need a real coach to help you get to the next level.

Then believe you can get there.

You can.

Dedicated to YOUR Success,
Aaron

CHAPTER 1

READ THIS *BEFORE* YOU HIRE A COACH

"It takes courage to grow up and become who you really are."
—*E.E. Cummings*

All industries should come with a guidebook of questions to ask and topics you need to be concerned with to best protect you. That's why I wrote this book. The self-development industry is in dire need of it. I'll get more into that in Chapter 2 when I discuss the massive explosion of the coaching industry and how NOTHING exists to help you navigate it without losing thousands of dollars and wasting your time and energy.

Until now.

I want you to use this book anytime you are considering hiring a coach in any capacity. Keep it handy.

Understand, I am not against hiring good coaches.

I am against hiring scam coaches who want your money and will drop-kick you as soon as they get it.

So, yes, hire a coach when you need one, but do the work I am about to lay out for you to get a good one that will pay off.

You should also use this book to make coaching investments better, more thought out, vetted, and logical. If you hire anyone based on emotion and not logic, you've got a bigger problem. When you are looking to improve yourself, the biggest lesson you will ever learn is logic. Math must trump every emotion.

This is inner work that not everyone wants to do.

But you're going to do it, right?

That's what I thought.

Let's start by talking about the areas of coaching you need to know about.

YOUR RESPONSIBILITIES TO YOUR COACH

You're hiring a coach.

Not a babysitter.

Your coach will expect you to put some mental and physical effort into this new relationship.

If you are wondering why, despite shoveling out a ton of cash for a coach, it's not working, you need to figure out what they aren't telling you about networking, showing up, and leveraging your leveling up.

YOUR COACH IS NOT YOUR BUDDY

One of the hardest things to watch is people who join these groups and think they have a brand-new friend in the coach when they are really a client. If you join the group because you want to call your coach your friend, you look unintelligent, and that's no way for the people whose impressions you care about to see you.

If gaining another friend is your mindset, you don't need a coach. Try increasing your networking instead. Or join a bowling league. Honestly, do anything but hire a coach.

I want this book to be the only investment in coaching you make right now. No matter how lonely you may feel running your business, loneliness is never a reason to hire anyone, whether it's a coach or another team member.

When you hire someone feeling that way, you won't get your money's worth. If you remember anything from this book, let it be that you must be in the right headspace before signing a coaching agreement.

EVERYONE'S A COACH

Despite all the negative content we're going to cover, I want you to know that there is helpful coaching information out there. Find it, and you can use it to elevate your business.

But how do you find it in the self-development industry when everyone who has lost 30 pounds or read coaching books and felt a "calling" is suddenly a coach?

There's a huge difference between getting coached and coaching someone else.

There's also a huge difference between experiencing a tiny bit of success and being qualified to teach because of that success.

Good coaches police themselves and know when they are qualified to offer mentorship and when they have more work to do. The best coaches I have met were never motivated by money and genuinely wanted to help people. They wanted to right a wrong in an industry. After gaining expertise in solving problems in the real world, they used that knowledge to help others coming up the path behind them. Remember, in coaching, there are NO LEVELS. There are only people further down the path from you. No one is above anyone else.

Check out these examples of two "coaches" doing it wrong in varying industries.

1. Are you familiar with the realtor who is suddenly a "success" coach because he sold a house once? Or maybe the "fitness coach" who used to be a stay-at-home mom, but then she dropped 20 pounds and pivoted to become a trainer because "fitness is her passion." I could go on and on, but the people who join coaching for their flavor of the month hobby are obvious. Ninety-nine percent are unsuccessful.

2. This example concerns groups of people who network together to bolster each other's success. They always speak at each other's "conferences and events" so they can build credibility and get booked to speak at big engagements with tons of speakers. Pay close attention, and you will notice it is always the same dudes peddling the same trash to each other's "followings." When they do this, they add layers to the deception. These people are smart; they know the audience and industry, although they never truly add tactical guidance you can use. They talk a mean game—because that's really their business, not helping you—so watch out.

As a brilliant coach of mine once told me, "If more than 5% of a coach's income comes from coaching and not real-world businesses, RUN."

If you feel like I am talking about you at any time in this book, it's not personal. If the shoe fits, sit back and ask yourself how you can do better as a coach and provide real value. I am not specifically calling anyone out, nor do I believe anyone is truly trying to be malicious and evil. But we all know there are people — a vast majority who have never built anything (and that's okay) — trying to be coaches. But you should never teach people about what you have never experienced. That's FRAUD.

IF YOU'RE DESPERATE, YOU'RE ON THEIR RADAR

Desperate so-called coaches are on the prowl. They see you, and you're on their email lists. You have a target on your head. They come at you and overwhelm you, and then you have no idea who to work with and who's worth it.

I hate not only that people (who might not even know better — that's a whole other story) take your money and time, but that so many people play at being a true influencer. When they do that, they only hurt people. They set them back. They confuse them and give the rest of the industry with good, caring coaches a bad rap.

That wannabe coach doesn't need to do much. Just throw up some media that depicts them owning the "right" car, wearing knock-offs of the "right" clothes, all posed outside the "right" mansion. And it works. People rush to them like they are in a race to divest themselves of their savings.

Their fake profiles inspire other lowlifes who only see dollar signs, and then there are more "coaches" to contend with.

It's easy for these "influencers" to make a name for themselves.

They prey on your deepest needs.

Without even realizing why … you want the trendy clothes they're modeling because you think they'll impress certain people. When they give you the praise you're hungry for, it feels like validation—just what you have been hoping to hear because you can't get it from yourself. If this is you, you don't need a coach; you need a boost of self-confidence.

RESEARCH FIRST

When you are looking for a coach, and you hear or read something that doesn't make sense, research it. If an opportunity seems too good to be true, it probably is. Sometimes we want so much to belong that we ignore what we should do to ensure we are making a wise decision.

We may want to be friends with guys like Gary Vee, Uncle G. (Grant Cardone), Ed Mylett, Andy Frisella, etc., but we shouldn't and don't deserve it. We haven't earned our seat at that table and, frankly, would embarrass ourselves if we found ourselves sitting there.

Imagine you are the age of your business. I may be 18 years old in fitness, but I'm only 5-plus years old as an entrepreneur. How old are you in your respective field?

Now ask yourself this…

Why would a 25-year-old wanna hang out with a five-year-old?

They wouldn't.

Maybe they'd get together on the holidays or at events occasionally. Here's another example: If you are a child, you might have a bomb babysitter, but you will never be invited to their house to chill, have a beer, watch the game, and talk shop.

Because YOU ARE FIVE YEARS OLD.

Yet, we see this all the time in the "game." We see people who haven't been at their business very long trying to be friends with people they can't hold a conversation with and don't deserve.

Do this, and it not only hurts your chances down the road, makes you look like a fool, and is annoying, but it also deters your focus from where it should be.

My main friends in my coaching group where I try to add value are 3-10-year-olds. These people are in the same class of entrepreneurship and are going through the same challenges as me and can help me solve real problems—and I can help them with their problems.

This is why researching where you will be networking is so key—because you are not just hiring that coach; you are hiring all the people around them. READ THAT AGAIN!!

That calls for hefty background checks to make sure you get into an organization that's the most advantageous to you.

Always play at your level and with kids your age. Eventually, you will be with the 20-year-olds. While you may think that being friends and buddies with the older kids in business is cool, remember that as you grow, evolve, and add years to your business age, so do the people around you. Eventually, that group of 3-10 year-olds will be the 25-year-olds everyone else wants to be around. It just takes time, and you cannot manipulate time. You HAVE to remain patient as you grow up and evolve.

My wife and I say the same thing to our kids. My six-year-old wants to drive and be a grown-up, but behind the wheel, he would hurt people. He isn't old enough, so he doesn't get to drive the car. It would be reckless to let him.

Grow up, learn, and play with kids your age. We learn this principle when we are young and forget its importance as we move into future chapters.

NO BARRIER TO ENTRY

The coaching and self-development industry has no barrier to entry, which is a good and bad thing. More people can get into this industry to build a brand and make something of themselves. When a person who actually cares about what they are offering is at the helm, that's awesome. But when a twisted person takes control and can make dollar signs out of your emotions, that's not cool. Steer clear.

VETTING MYSELF

In the following chapters, I will explain my experience to you and share what I learned from watching an entire industry explode into the multi-billions. It is a complete bastardization of what it started out to be—which is why we have the problems we do.

In an explosion, people get burned. That has been the case in the self-development industry. A bunch of people flooded the market who claim to know how to scale your business, teach you marketing, and turn you into a Kardashian overflowing with sponsor money hitting your bank account. You should know, it's extremely hard to earn money that way. Almost impossible. It also takes years.

Because I believe it's essential for coaches to vet themselves, I will do just that and explain how I leveraged my six-figure business to become eight figures and now a nearly nine-figure buyout.

Any coach you want to hire should be open about their history and their missteps and successes.

Everything I am sharing with you that I have done is factual, and I'm not just pumping up numbers to make myself feel good and get your attention. You can verify every word here if you want to Google or DuckDuckGo me.

MAKE THE DECISION FOR YOURSELF ... NOT SO THAT YOU FIT IN

Get in the habit of weighing your options and choosing the right solution for your circumstances. Before you fork out one buck to a costly coaching group or mentor, it's critical that you understand how they work, what you'll get out of them, and how to best utilize them.

Some people use these groups as a lead magnet. I don't have a digital product, so I needed to find out what made the most sense to invest in as the owner of brick-and-mortar gyms. I wasn't going to join any group until I determined there was a benefit to my business and me.

PLAY BY THE RULES FIRST

We've all heard the saying: "Your network is your net worth."

While this statement is true, it is misleading.

Your network is the net of your *actual work,* not the number of people you have access to and can talk to.

The real players in this game respect the work. The action. The result.

People at the highest levels want to see what you do, not who you know. They want to see what you are producing, not what you are contemplating.

If you want to be respected in your network, build something first. Then maybe you'll catch the eye of someone a little further up the ladder.

Business isn't an opinion of when you can move to the next level; it's an equation. PERIOD. You must humble yourself to the math and logic or be part of the 90-something percent who fail.

The successful people you admire had to fall on their faces and pay their dues. In doing so, they established credibility. Then they could bend the rules a little since people knew what they were doing. Finally, they could break them and rewrite them to best fit them. But you don't get to do that right out of the gate. You have to pay your dues and work first.

OFFER AND TAKE VALUE

This little piece is lost on many people. Many people make connections but have no idea what to do with those relationships. They don't know how to serve their network and haven't done any work to learn how to provide any sort of meaningful interaction.

Like any relationship, networking is a two-way street.

You're not going to wring the crap out of your circle without offering anything in return.

You offer value, and you take it. It's that simple.

WHAT ARE YOUR DOLLARS BUYING?

As you read through this book, I want you to feel confident about where to put your dollars. Make sure they go out the door buy you something that you need.

Ask yourself questions about your prospective coaches:

- What else are they sharing and doing to improve themselves?

- How are they modeling what winning looks like?

Think about who you're following, get to know what they stand for and their virtues and values. Do they match what you want? Only when you can determine this should you fork over money.

HAVE THE COURAGE TO WALK AWAY

Finally, don't be afraid to walk away. There's nothing wrong with deciding a coach is not for you after working with them. That's okay. You are not bound by blood to the coach you choose.

No quality coach has a contract that locks you into working with them for a specific length of time. People and good coaches have evolved. Any contract you sign should be a month-to-month value exchange. Unless you are paying for one-on-one attention that guarantees you a set program, I can't imagine why you would ever sign a contract. Even then—if your prospective coach insists this is what they need, I would fight it.

Make sure you know what you are getting into and what will be required of you.

IN CLOSING...

I wrote this book to set a screwed-up industry straight and return the power to you when you are ready to hire a coach.

Now, make that commitment to yourself not to spend a penny until you've finished every page of this book. You'll be glad you did!

CHAPTER 2

DON'T BE ME

"Income seldom exceeds personal development."
—Jim Rohn

If I told you that the global CBD industry was projected to be $3.5B by the end of 2021 and $13.4B by 2028, would you be surprised?[1]

It might be shocking, but it makes sense if we take into account all we know about the industry—where CBD is sold and how our neighbors are even hocking this stuff.

Knowing that figure, what would you guess the self-development industry is worth? And what do you think the projections for the self-development industry over the next few years are?

STAGGERING STATS ABOUT THE INDUSTRY

According to Grandview Research, in 2019, the self-development industry made $38.28B globally and is on track to reach $56.6B by 2027![2]

---

[1] "Cannabidiol Market Growth Analysis Report, 2021-2028." Cannabidiol Market Growth Analysis Report, 2021-2028. Accessed January 16, 2022.
https://www.grandviewresearch.com/industry-analysis/cannabidiol-cbd-market
[2] "Personal Development Market Size Report, 2020-2027." Personal Development Market Size Report, 2020-2027. Accessed January 16, 2022.
https://www.grandviewresearch.com/industry-analysis/personal-development-market.

It's shocking, but over the past few years, this industry has positively blown up.

When industries expand so quickly, we lose the ability to regulate them, which is another reason I wrote this book. It's the perfect storm of people wanting help and feeling desperate to make foundational changes in their lives and coach vultures just waiting to swoop in and snatch up all their money.

I wasted thousands of dollars on coaches who did nothing for me, and I don't want that to happen to you.

MY STORY

I share my personal story with you because I need to show you the type of information I expect you to uncover in researching others.

So, I have to go first. This is the kind of integrity I want you to search for in your coaches—the ones who walk the talk.

I made a lot of mistakes in this industry, but you don't have to make the same ones I did—or the mistakes other people made—once you know what they are.

When I was figuring out what help I needed with my company, I noticed people would buy tickets to conferences, get all excited at the live event, and then be crestfallen when the show started with only 12 people on stage. I saw many people falling prey to this type of marketing, who were getting only a fraction of the value that they could be buying—what a waste of their time and money.

HOW I LEARNED ABOUT COACHING

I started my journey because of Grant Cardone—good Ol' Uncle G. When I learned what he was about, I moved to Florida and even rented a high-rise apartment just like him.

When he held his first conference at the Diplomat in Miami, I was in. I paid for a mid-grade ticket, heard some great speakers, watched Russell Brunson sell everyone ClickFunnels, and everyone else sell their coaching programs. Grant and Jared even came out and said, "We want you to be broke when you leave because you spent every penny on the speakers' programs."

The only two men who didn't sell were Andy Frisella and Tim Grover. I am now honored to call both of them my friends and mentors. They entered the stage and blew away the crowd by offering real value and not wanting anything in return. Andy and Tim made such an impression that I signed up for the next event in Vegas. At that time, I had just opened my second gym.

In Vegas, I heard the same regurgitation that so many coaches spew out, including the same ClickFunnels sales pitch verbatim. While I was there, I bought a couple of other "life-changing" programs that didn't amount to anything. But this time, three men stood out to me.

The original two, Andy and Tim, who I brought my team to see, and a third, Ed Mylett, were unforgettable. By the time the conference was over, I was appalled at the amount of selling and information gathering going on for the price we'd paid. Still, I shrugged it off and moved on. But on the way home, I realized I wasn't taking much else away. I went back to Florida trying to figure out how to expand my businesses—but none the wiser and a little poorer.

Then an email came from Ed's and Andy's camp announcing that they'd launched Arete Syndicate. I had been chosen out of 10,000 people to be one of their members—for no reason. I was a nobody and very fortunate. Feeling lucky, I went all-in on the investment, and to this day, they have helped me grow and realize strategies to implement in my business that I had no idea of. Their connections alone have 100X'd my businesses.

No joke.

I've gone from owning two gyms to outselling the biggest names in my industry in franchising in year one. These men taught me the fundamentals that will allow my business to last in a highly competitive field.

I have never looked back.

I love Uncle G. for introducing me to the men I call my mentors. I appreciate every dollar I've spent with him and that he started me down the path. So, thank you, Grant, for being a part of my journey, even if only for the lessons learned.

After hearing about how I found my coaches and made that investment, ask yourself: *Besides spending money on a coach, what else could I do with $10,000 infused into my business?*

Why would you not spend that money on an investment that would pay your business back?

When I joined the Arete coaching program, I'd scaled as much as I could by myself but had no idea what direction to go. I didn't know enough about distribution, how to change my processes until they fit what I was doing, and I couldn't see that my product was inferior. This is the difference between being ignorant and an idiot. Ignorance is not knowing what you don't know, and being an idiot is knowing what you should do and still choosing not to do it.

In short: I didn't know what I didn't know.

My goal in joining the Arete Syndicate was to find someone who could help me save money on taxes. I was wildly successful and found a guy who reduced my estimated tax bill from $90k to $32k. That was enough for me. I was in and interested in learning who else I could meet to help me in my business and life.

Next, I met a book coach and editor to assist me with my first book, *The Darkside Dichotomy: Unleashing Your True Power Through Pain.*

Then I learned about more effective marketing for my business and how to launch my third location more efficiently. I did that with a client list of 462, which at the time was mind-blowing to me—but was nothing compared to what was coming down the pipeline, all because I hired the right coaches.

Arete made me more excellent at what I was already doing, and I improved in many ways due to the insane knowledge of the members representing all kinds of industries. Every time I went to a meeting at Arete, I went with a goal in mind, whether it was optimizing high-quality leads for less money or staffing the services I needed—an attorney for asset protection, an investment advisor, or someone to coach me on exit strategies. When I went looking, I always found a resource. I have been able to apply what Arete taught me about finances to improve and grow my business.

The more I grew and leveled up, the more impressive the experts at the higher levels were. The people I met at levels five and six were far more valuable to my business than those on level two.

I'm living proof that if you keep putting in the years and remain loyal to a group that really puts out the value, it will truly show you what "10X" means.

CHAPTER 3

QUESTIONS TO ASK BEFORE YOU GIVE A COACH ANY MONEY

"Don't go broke trying to look rich."
—Unknown

READ THIS *BEFORE* HANDING OVER YOUR CREDIT CARD.

First...

Get into the habit of asking questions of yourself and your potential coach before you agree to work with anyone. You will save money.

But don't just ask the questions; do your research.

Even if you don't like what the research uncovers, decide who you will hire based on facts.

I'm not telling you to DM (direct message) or bug super high-level people. You probably won't get a response, and if they even see your message, your first impression won't be positive.

For the love of all things holy, RESEARCH before you ask anyone —a coach or their team—anything.

If you ask an intelligent, well-thought-out question that you can't find the answer to in their content, messaging, or offering, THEN ask.

Nothing looks worse to these coaches—especially the real ones—than being a time-waster. Follow them for a while, understand their businesses and value. If you discover they can help you in an area where you need to improve, THEN start the conversation with them.

Better yet, if they have staff who can help you, ask them. Authentic coaches deal with millions of people in their massive followings, so don't waste their time and bug them. Best-case scenario, your message won't register, and they won't remember you. Worst-case scenario, it will, and they will.

The answers you uncover should make you feel empowered by your decisions. And don't lie about the research you discover. If someone you want to work with is doing a terrible job, but all your entrepreneur friends are working with them, don't rationalize their below-average results. It is what it is, and your job is to accept it and move on. Your friends don't have your needs, and you don't have theirs.

The following questions have helped me determine who the best people are to add to my professional and self-development network. I have used them as I have grown from being a fitness trainer to owning a gym then multiple gyms with fitness trainers.

I've learned who people say they are and what they do can be very different.

So, make sure you answer the following questions to protect yourself.

KNOW THESE FACTS ABOUT YOUR COACH AND YOURSELF

What do they do?

Get very specific in identifying this answer. Is this person a business coach? A coach for personal trainers? Do they work with financial advisors?

Make sure this person provides an easy-to-understand service based on what they're doing and what they say. Your research should prove this. If you are looking for a personal trainer, you would expect to find a person talking about fitness, nutrition, exercise, etc. It's not hard to figure out if someone is misrepresenting themselves or if they have recently started coaching. Get the info you need until you feel like you no longer need to research.

What is their Return on Investment (ROI)?

In other words, what have their other clients made back in terms of money, knowledge, and time from their investment? Do they have greater visibility in the marketplace? Did they learn how to scale their business effectively, and can they apply that strategy to their current companies? After making any investment, you should be able to definitively state, "I paid X amount of dollars, and this is what I got in return." You should also be able to read other's results with that same amount of precision.

What is my goal?

So many people sign up for masterminds and attach to coaches, but they don't consider how they will apply what they are about to learn to their business.

Ask yourself:

- What am I going to do with this new knowledge?

- How can I apply it to my business?

- How will I allow it to improve me?

- Have I looked at my business and determined how I want to change it and make it stronger?

Before you begin shopping around for a coach, trainer, or mastermind developer, have a goal. Then match your goal to a reputable person who can help you achieve it.

When you answer this question, be honest with yourself. People often tell themselves the truths they *believe* are true. Sometimes people spend money to hire others or work with them because it makes them feel like they're doing something—although they might just be spinning their wheels.

If you clam up when you try to explain what your coach does, it's a sign that you don't know a lot about that person or what to expect from your investment.

Make sure you can identify your goal and find, vet and research your coach In other words, do the work. Then take the results from working with the coach and apply them to your goal.

Once you know your goal, examine your patterns.

Do you buy products or services but never do anything with them? If so, it's time to figure out why that is. Address this, and you can change the course of your personal development.

Now, let me add this….

Once you do commit, please GO ALL IN.

When I first joined Arete, at the first summit, we got on a boat and headed to Ed's mansion. There I was surrounded by Tim Grover and 50 other badass dudes who were wearing clothes that cost more than I was worth.

I knew exactly one guy, so I sat next to him and mostly kept to myself. I didn't really network at all and went home petrified, feeling like I didn't belong.

Given the price tag of the original syndicate and the fact that I was closing on our house, I knew I had to do more.

When the time came for the next event, I went with the goal to talk to an expert to help me with my taxes, and I was successful in saving thousands of dollars. This underscores my point that you will get more out of your masterminds and events when you go there with a goal.

At the third event, I met my marketing guy and BOOM! Now, we work together in all our franchisees and my companies.

Shortly after that, I met my ghostwriter, and two books later, here we are. We've got it down to a process now, going back and forth, writing the whole damn thing word for word together. She's amazing and can combat my ADD.

I've also met a bunch of men who bought our company franchises —because I went all in.

They believed in my franchises so much that they wanted to be a part of it. They've watched me work, seen me apply and implement the coaching I've learned, evaluate my results, adjust fire when needed, and ultimately win.

DO NOT JOIN GROUPS AND SIT ON THE SIDELINES. SUCK EVERY LITTLE MOLECULE OF VALUE OUT OF YOUR EXCHANGE!

It is YOUR responsibility to utilize the group and to bring your goals with you so you can find the resources needed to meet them. It is not the coach's job to hold your hand and *hope* you take your responsibilities seriously. If that's your plan, you need a babysitter *and* a cheerleader, *not* a coach.

Join with the intention to participate and grab opportunities within that group. Speak up with the permission of the admins. Comment and add value to the other members. If it's allowed, help people outside the group, but don't go on a hunt to close them.

On that note, make sure you read the rules and understand the deal-breakers. If you're not supposed to prospect people outside the group, it's not worth bending the rules to force a sale when you'll probably get booted.

The old saying is: "The squeaky wheel gets the grease," so ask questions and post. Let people know you are a resource for them. Business will ensue *then*. We want to make sure that people know we're there, that we're participating and interested in what's going on —that we're not shy about wanting to know more. Also, when you're an active member of a group, the admin is more likely to notice you. That's a definite bonus!

But don't go crazy, either, and expect the admin to know who you are and send a bunch of resources your way after uttering the perfect comment or asking one question. It's not likely. You're better off accepting that fact right now.

Work at networking like you work at your job or entrepreneurship.

Don't we all need the same coach?

Ask me that question in person, and I'll stare at you like you've got two heads.

There are different types of coaches. I named a couple of these specialists at the beginning of this book, so I know you know the answer.

No, and duh.

Before you pick your coach, you need to know:

- How should I spend my money?
- What do I need?
- Do I need help with a Facebook group?
- What is my industry, and who can give me the best help?

I know you have more questions than that, so go ahead and write them down. Then work on finding the most effective solutions for you.

Only you know the answers to these questions. Take your time and make sure you get these answers right.

My world is the fitness world. As I explore coaching opportunities in that industry, I ask myself: *What do I need? Does it make sense to join this mastermind to help me with my current challenge? Do I need help with networking? Do I need guidance in rewriting my processes?*

Since starting my coaching journey, I've learned how important it is to answer these questions.

When I was in the habit of not asking them of myself, I depleted any resources I could have used to lead me to the right solutions. I am now committed to finding the answers that give me the most bang for my buck. Whenever I need to hire someone new, I ask myself similar questions about my goals, so my head is clear. I know what I'm getting into and what I can reasonably expect in return.

**Remember, this is an investment.
Good ones produce a return;
great ones can change everything.**

This last question pertains to you if you are trying to get a coaching business up and running:

Are you playing at being an entrepreneur or influencer?

Have you changed your title in a heartbeat, jumped on the product-selling bandwagon without having a genuine interest, joined an MLM, or do you hop from industry to industry? Do you refuse to say that you are a salesperson and try and get out of doing the unsexy work of the business in favor of snapping pics and posting on social media? If so, you might be a fake influencer, and you certainly don't understand the real work that goes into running a legit business.

Playing at anything is not being it.

You might suspect you are getting away with it, but genuine businesspeople know you're hiding behind a veil of shame, secrecy, and lies. It doesn't take much to lift that veil and expose you. If I were you, I would be afraid, very afraid.

As a person who has done the work, put in the time, learned the lessons, and lasted through the hard times, as well as felt the pain and powered through it, I know you're fake. So don't think you're clever.

Even though I may know more than others in this industry, I realize I'm not as clever as people at the top. They see through bull way faster than I do, and they never spend the same dollar twice. Once they evaluate you, they will likely hold that notion of who you are unless something drastic changes.

That's the good and bad news of first impressions. When it comes to coaches, they can take you to the top or tank you, so don't allow someone to formulate an opinion about you until YOU are ready. It's not worth wasting an opportunity with a bona fide leader in your industry if you provide no value or have no legitimacy.

Until you have the chops, play at the smaller tables with kids your age in business. At that level, you can mess up and learn lessons that will eventually get you an invite into an exclusive network. It just takes time, consistency, growth, and a solid track record—all of which require real patience.

Don't forget that being an authentic person in this space has nothing to do with what you're driving, where you live, or where you're vacationing. That fun stuff comes as a *side effect* of running a legit business, but it shouldn't be the driving factor behind what you're doing—the driving factor should be helping people.

Genuine coaches' content doesn't have much to do with fake people either. Their content has to do with you. It has to do with people searching for how to scale their business, trusting the people they've hired, and automating their processes, etc. Genuine coaches create content to help *you* solve problems. The work they do every day revolves around their clients.

Conversely, fake influencers get up every day and think, *How can I look cool? How can I look hot? How can I get a bunch of likes, comments, and shares so that I feel good about myself?* (Although they likely won't have any idea *why* they want all that attention. Some part of them will just register that they do.) From the outside looking in, you can see that they stink of their own bull—that they somehow believe. Stay far away.

If you're not coaching for the right reasons, you're hurting the industry. You're hurting people who want to work hard to get their business out there and keep the entrepreneurial spirit alive.

So, knock it off!

CHAPTER 4

DO YOU EVEN NEED A COACH?

"The first and most important person
you must believe in is yourself."
— Tori Sorenson

Knowing where you are excelling and where to channel improvements can change the trajectory of your life and business, so read this chapter carefully.

You will also want to check out the self-assessment PDF form I've created for you on my Instagram page @aaronnash20.

It looks like this:

BURNED STOP GETTING CONNED BY FAKE COACHES
IN THE PERSONAL DEVELOPMENT EXPLOSION.   **SELF ASSESSMENT**

NAME   **BUSINESS**   **AMOUNT TO INVEST (COACHING, GROUP TRAINING, ETC.).**

INDUSTRY LEADERS

1.   4.

2.   5.

3.

INDUSTRY LEADERS STRENGTHS (I.E., MARKETING, CULTURE, ETC.).

MY BUSINESS STRENGTHS (I.E., MARKETING).

HOW CAN I SPEND THAT SAME AMOUNT ON MY STRENGTHS?

HOW CAN I SPEND THAT SAME AMOUNT ON MY WEAKNESSES?

BEST ROI IF THE MONEY I SPENT WORKS?:

WORST ROI IF THE MONEY I SPENT DID NOT PRODUCE RESULTS?:

DO YOU EVEN NEED A COACH?

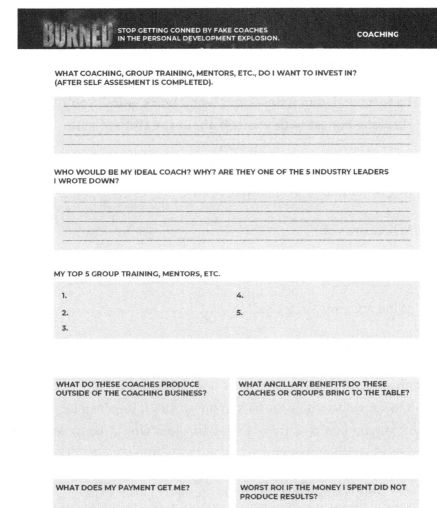

BURNED STOP GETTING CONNED BY FAKE COACHES
IN THE PERSONAL DEVELOPMENT EXPLOSION.
COACHING

WHAT COACHING, GROUP TRAINING, MENTORS, ETC., DO I WANT TO INVEST IN?
(AFTER SELF ASSESMENT IS COMPLETED).

WHO WOULD BE MY IDEAL COACH? WHY? ARE THEY ONE OF THE 5 INDUSTRY LEADERS
I WROTE DOWN?

MY TOP 5 GROUP TRAINING, MENTORS, ETC.

1.   4.
2.   5.
3.

WHAT DO THESE COACHES PRODUCE
OUTSIDE OF THE COACHING BUSINESS?

WHAT ANCILLARY BENEFITS DO THESE
COACHES OR GROUPS BRING TO THE TABLE?

WHAT DOES MY PAYMENT GET ME?

WORST ROI IF THE MONEY I SPENT DID NOT
PRODUCE RESULTS?

WHY IS THIS INVESTMENT BETTER THAN USING THE MONEY FOR MY OWN BUSINESS?

When completing this form, be honest.

Don't inflate your numbers.

The form and your assessment won't work unless you're brutally honest with yourself about the state of your business.

Among other things, you need to know:

- Where are you?

- How close are you to reaching your goals?

- What are your struggles?

- Are they in your marketing, culture, or systems, etc.?

When answering these questions and ranking yourself, compare yourself to someone who's the best in the world. If they're a ten, what are you? Maybe you're a two. If so, your goal would be to reach a three, not a nine. Wherever you are on the scale, aim to go up one level.

While completing this exercise, research the expert you've identified. Figure out why they're good. Who runs their company or companies? Do they have coaching programs? What else can you uncover about them that would make a difference in your life?

Maybe you will be surprised to learn that you don't need a coach yet.

Regardless, be prepared to answer these questions.

GET OFF THE BANDWAGON

I hate to tell you this, but if you want to hang out with all your friends who have signed up to work with the same coach, it doesn't mean that you will get the same value from them.

Do not hire a coach because you don't want to be alone or you need someone to tell you how wonderful you and your choices are.

Besides, let's get real. Owning a business is isolating.

If you're getting started, you're probably feeling that pain. But here's a hard fact: If you're going to last, you need to get used to that. You will make the decisions and have to sit with your indecisions. You will be responsible for weighing the direction you want to go and how to course-correct when you go the wrong way. Sure, you can talk to people about what you are dealing with, but no one else will have the same insight or attachment as you. They cannot alleviate that sinking feeling in your gut—nothing can do that.

The only thing that works is muscling through it. So, sit in the misery, the indecision, the doubt, all of it. When you're used to that, you'll get your head on straight. You'll be tougher and able to assess what you really need and what you don't. Even better, once you can see those truths, you'll have the strength to walk away from anything that doesn't serve you.

WHERE DO YOU SUCK?

Knowing where you suck is a big deal. You can look at your areas that need improving and match up to a coach. Or … you might uncover that you want to go in a different direction and will hire a different service.

The point is you need to know what you're up against, so figure out your weaknesses before making major business decisions.

If you don't know how to determine your weaknesses, write down the areas in business that you feel matter the most.

Next, decide who is the best in those areas. Consider Andy Frisella's culture and systems, Ed Mylett's vision casting, Gary Vee's creativity, Billy Gene's marketing, David Goggins' mental toughness, etc.

Understand that even if you think they are a ten, none of them would assess themselves that way. So as we complete this exercise, let's assume they all rank at a 9.5 on our scale. Where are you in relation to them?

For instance, if Andy is a 9.5 at systems creation or building great team members, what makes him and his company so good at it? Is it their training programs? Their "start from the bottom" approach? Their pay structures? Their hours and schedules? Their core values? How they hire and fire? Their system for replicating jobs and building people into positions? Their meeting schedule? Their headquarters that currently rivals any place on planet Earth? Their interview process? Identify what it is.

We want to break it down to show you how much you don't know and the areas where you likely can improve right off the bat.

If you know you need a better team and systems for attracting and hiring good people so you can turn them into great people, joining Arete is easily the right decision. But you don't need to attend an event and spend five figures right away when you join. Participating in the calls each week is enough and will cover what you need to know thoroughly—if you listen with intent. Check out the free info available to you, too, like what's shared on the podcasts.

You always want to assess and find out where your potential coach gives away information. Is it through a podcast, Facebook, Instagram, TikTok, LinkedIn, etc.? There are great people everywhere taking real-world action and teaching about topics you want to learn about. Luckily, most of them give out free content. The trick is to do the assessment, know what you are focused on, and let your Reticular Activating System do the rest. If you don't get it, look it up.

This is why you need to be honest and use the Portnoy scale, which calls for very specific numbers. Don't use round numbers like 6, 7, 8, and so on. Those are rookie numbers. Use exact numbers like 3.4, 6.2, etc. Doing so will help you realize two facts about yourself: 1) how far you have to go, and 2) you aren't the worst on Earth, either.

Knowing your numbers helps you logically decide where you suck the most. Once you've figured out where you suck, it's still not time to hire a coach.

Stop.

Now decide if you would value being great in this area where you are struggling or if it's a better option to hire someone who excels there. *Only* if you deem your level of competence detrimental to your business growth should you seek to improve.

After that assessment, guess what?

You're still not ready to hire a coach.

Don't go straight to IG to find the next neophyte who thinks they have a clue. Research online and in books. Find authors. This deep dive is cheap and easy and will build *real* skills faster and better than any class. Once you have read six books on the subject and immersed yourself in the skill set, THEN you can decide who to hire, why, and what you will get out of it.

If you go straight to the coach without doing any of the needed research, you will not understand what they do. Gain your competency through literature before hiring an expert.

Never stop being a book student. Every single successful person I know reads AT LEAST one book per month. If you don't, look at your life. If you're happy, cool. If you're not, read MORE.

HIRE TWO, FIRE ONE

I once hired a marketing guy even though I already had a marketing guy working for me because I thought he could improve the number of leads coming in. Plus, this allowed me to learn more about my marketing guy.

My "Hire two, fire one" method is another way to do research, and it solved a need in my business without consulting a coach.

If you think this will work in your situation, I invite you to try it!

I discovered that I could pit these guys against each other to see who was going to outwork the other. Whoever won, I kept in the business.

First, I played one against the other out of curiosity.

Since each of them had the same budget, it seemed like the playing field was leveled. With that handled, I sat back and watched the results to see who was doing what differently. This process also kept my current marketer honest.

I figured if he was doing his job, his results shouldn't change if I brought on another person. If anything, since he knew I'd hired another person in his position, he would work harder.

I needed to look inward to my business and see what I could resolve myself in this instance. I didn't need anything else but marketing help—and that's exactly what I got.

Why would I buy more services than I needed?

Why would you?

This is one of the benefits of getting specific—you know where to spend your money.

The advantage of "hire two, fire one" works in any area of your business. In real life, there are winners and losers. Period.

If you operate your business on being inclusive, hiring people based on color, orientation, religion, what genitals they have this week, or what pronouns they use, you are an idiot.

Maybe that sounds harsh, but the best solution for your business is always to hire the best and hire two people for each position. As I've gone over with you, the best one wins; the one who doesn't perform as well learns and grows or has an ego problem and takes himself out of the picture.

If the original guy wins, I never tell him. But if the second guy wins, I tell the first guy he has 30 days to outperform the winner. Of course, I explain to him what I had done.

In business, you need to keep competing. The worst thing that can happen if you run this scenario is finding two great people, which is a home run. Your company will win faster because your team becomes your biggest asset. If you think labor is a liability, you will lose. For real company and real growth, you need people.

Remember, you can go fast alone, but you can't go far. You are only as good as your team, and continuing to invest, improve, and have healthy competition inside your business is KEY to growth.

REFER TO THE MATH

Before I go on, you need to better understand how my mind works. I am not married to any decision in my business. I look at the math. Period. And I accept my choices.

I could have let my ego block me, but I chose to accept that I needed to make another pivot in my million-mile business journey. I accepted that I had so much further to go.

The biggest error people make is inflating their egos and abilities instead of accepting they are a newbie and have a lot to learn.

**I approach my business like my marriage.
It always comes first.**

My commitment to my business is non-negotiable. It also always comes first because the math shows me what decision to make.

My marriage is also a math equation. I've never met a woman worth half of my current shit, so I am all in for my wife. As your net worth improves, keep that in mind. When asked how he stayed married for 50 years, the great Lou Holtz once said, "It's cheaper to keep her."

Nothing comes above doing what is best for my business. If somebody or something is not right for it or an investment is not panning out, I have no qualms walking away and cutting ties to preserve it.

The good news is that "Hire two, fire one" doesn't only pertain to your marketing.

Don't be afraid to hire another guy to do your taxes and bookkeeping or handle any other area of your business.

I tell that story to illustrate that I knew what I needed. That is what I went after, and that is what I hired for. I didn't look at the leads coming in and say, "I must hire somebody who's going to make me feel good about myself ... or about my business ... or about where I'm spending my money ... or about where my business has grown to." I took any feelings I had about the situation out of it. I encourage you to learn how to do that, too.

I know it's hard when your identity is wrapped up in your business, but you will never go the distance if you can't get out of your feelings and learn perspective. Acknowledge, plan, act.

CHAPTER 5

ACKNOWLEDGING AND ADDRESSING YOUR WEAKNESSES

"My strength and my weakness are twins in the same womb."
—Marge Piercy

If you are don't feel confident discussing your areas of improvement, let me help you out. Remember, we all have weaknesses, so let's not make a big deal about it. Just identify your weaknesses, make a plan to get better, or bring on someone who can do what you don't want to do or can't do.

Do any of these apply to you? Be honest, then get to work.

1. **Being weak in time management skills.**

   If you're lacking in this area, you don't need to join a group. Just grow up. You also don't need a coach or trainer to help you with your mindset. They're not your crutch. They won't guarantee your results.

   If you do the work, this poor excuse for a weakness will resolve itself.

2. **Not knowing the best coach to help you**.

I know from running my business and being a trainer that specific niches can benefit people the most. For instance, if you want to lose weight, I can advise you on that. I know what to tell you and how to guide you. But if you want to train for a marathon, even though I can give you some tips, you would be better off using a different trainer. This is a hyper niche.

Hyper niches are growing every day. If you can't find your hyper niche, congratulations! You just discovered one, and your business can be the first in it. Just kidding! Unless you are qualified to coach, don't do this.

We see hyper niches in various fields. If you work in marketing, maybe your specialty is automating your email content or social media responses. Maybe you focus on writing all the blogs for your business or a client. There are hyper niches in coaching as well, like business, life, sales, etc.

If your company specializes in a hyper niche, you might not want to sign with a coach who emphasizes a more general approach to what they're teaching. I'm not saying that you can't learn from them and take value from what they're sharing. But there will be times when you need somebody in your specialized industry or field to ensure they can give you the tips and tricks of what's worked for them.

My two best business advisors are guys in the same space as me. We don't compete because we know there is enough to go around. We help each other because we want to know what's working and how we can all get better. It's not about a low-level scorched earth mentality once you reach the higher levels. It's about improvement and teamwork. When you experience this, you'll know you are growing up in business.

3. **Struggling with overall enthusiasm.**

If you are fighting yourself to get your work done and/or complete certain tasks, maybe you don't like what you're doing or the core function of your business. Ask yourself, *Am I trying to push this rock up the hill? Can I even stand doing this every day? Do I feel passionate about my business?*

People start the wrong businesses all the time. They go all-in to what doesn't fulfill them. The worst thing you can do is try to find the excitement that you will never find—it just doesn't happen when you hate what you do. That's not a bad thing to say; it's a fact that you need to figure out what to do with and how you will change it.

Not liking your business might be why you are trying to reinvigorate it by buying your tenth coaching service and attending your hundredth mastermind.

If you know you hate your business, but you won't let yourself admit it, go ahead and say it out loud. You can't avoid hearing the truth if it comes out of your month, and you're forced to hear it. It also doesn't matter if you hate the business because you can always make a fresh start. Just go back to the drawing board.

You need self-motivation if you're an entrepreneur. If you don't have an innate enthusiasm, you won't succeed. Grueling tasks are ahead of you as an entrepreneur. You need to have passion, so you can complete them without burning out and failing. You might not like what I have to say, but at least you won't ever have to question if it's true!

To clarify, I'm not talking about the people who hate a specific *task*. Maybe you don't like doing social media, but you love speaking to clients. Maybe you don't like writing emails, but you dig managing people. Whatever your personal situation, you can overcome a little hatred over a to-do versus showing up for work every day and wanting to be anywhere but there.

Confucius said, "Do what you love, and you will never work a day in your life." He was full of crap. You won't love *everything*. That saying is misleading. It causes people to think there's something wrong with the way they feel about their business. It makes them think they should close up shop because they hate the handful of things they must do to keep the doors open. This isn't true. Please know there will be days you want to escape. There will be jobs you are not happy to do. That's normal.

If you can't stand your business, why waste another minute in it? Life's too short. It's time to figure out something else.

Passion gives you the initiative to learn and grow. It gives you the ability to get past the tasks you don't want to do so you can focus on the ones you enjoy.

In the fitness industry, I get all pumped up when I earn certificates, learn about new methods, and see others accomplish their goals. When I feel that way, I know I'm where I am supposed to be and that the people hitting their targets are where they belong, too.

If you're struggling to work in your business, think about the hobbies you love, whether it's playing board or video games or learning about sports cars. That's the kind of passion I'm talking about. It should be very evident in your business.

For those tasks you don't like to do, there's a very simple solution that I've already mentioned. Find somebody else who *loves* to do them.

There's nothing wrong with saying, "I don't like this chore, and I want somebody else to do it." It doesn't make you sound lazy; it makes you sound like you know what you want in your life. Understanding this can be tremendously helpful to the success of your business.

4. **Can you be self-accountable enough not to need a babysitter?**

Again, coaches are not babysitters. They don't guarantee results. A good coach would never put you or themselves in that position because the variables are too great. The people are too different, and the industries are too varied. Our backgrounds, experiences, genealogy, and mindsets are vastly different.

An effective coach will tell you what to do, but it is not their job to ensure you do it. Their job is to let you discover the best application for the knowledge they've taught you.

They will remind you of what's on your goal list, check in with you to see how it's going and if you need anything. But don't rely on your coach to keep track of what you are supposed to be doing. You are working with them to build skills—one of them is self-accountability.

5. **Piggybacking off weakness.**

Number one, if you don't have great time management skills, but blame the coach, we know who's responsible. Patient zero.

In this case, don't fool yourself. The reason you can't stay on track is that you don't want to do the work. You might feed yourself an excuse like, "I keep trying everything, but nothing is working."

When the truth is you haven't done the work. It's not that the coaching methodology isn't working. It's that you're not working. You MUST do the work. I will never sugarcoat that for you.

Don't expect to hire a good coach to lather you up with compliments and tell you how great you're doing if you're not staying on top of your plan. They will encourage and help you find your personal empowerment, but they will never, ever make you feel like you have to lean on them or depend on them to make you feel better—even if you do the work. They're going to call you out on your excuses. That's what makes them a good coach.

If you don't do your work, a caring coach will say, "I can see you didn't do what you were supposed to, so you are not going to achieve this result." Coaches don't guarantee the results in part because they cannot be sure you will do the work.

CHAPTER 6

DEFINING DIRECTION...
AND A LITTLE CLARITY

*"Your power to choose your direction of your life allows
you to reinvent yourself, to change your future,
and to powerfully influence the rest of creation."*
—*Stephen Covey*

After you've answered the questions in the following chapters and determined what you need, it's time to get after it. Maybe you need 1,000 followers, for instance. If that's the case, you probably don't need to hire a coach.

FITNESS COACHES

Let me speak from experience and tell you that if you're in the fitness industry and seeking 1,000 people, you might only need to find ten people who need to lose 30 pounds. Track with me here: You could work with them for free and document everything they're doing that's effective. After six to eight weeks, you'll see eight to ten great results. That's a fair success percentage when you assume what will likely happen: one guy might not do the work. A gal might've sprained her knee. Eighty percent is respectable. You can use those results to build your business.

When I see people who are realistic about what they've gone through, but they didn't have 100% success, I have huge respect for them. I don't want to hear all about the sunshine and puppies and unicorns. I want to hear the real, gritty facts: "Aaron, it was grueling, but I went through it. I've learned why I made this mistake. This strategy didn't work for this client, and here's why," are words I can work with—that your coach can work with.

**Those words help define the goals you want to hit.
Your failures should make your goals that much clearer.**

While you are in the midst of building a fitness brand, you can also get people to write testimonials for you. Word-of-mouth is always effective. Offer to work with clients for free until you can build a paying business from referrals. Soon, you'll have people coming to you saying, "I heard you were the guy/gal who's gonna help me lose 30 pounds." There's nothing stronger than social proof when you're trying to build a business.

If you want to become a coach, let me give you a word of caution. When working in the fitness and nutrition field, make sure you study diet and nutrition. Have an interest in it that fuels you to learn more and improve your clients' experiences with you.

Don't turn yourself into a fake person and say, "I didn't work out for a year, then I lost 40 pounds, and now I'm really good at it." Every Susie soccer mom can do this. That's why they all sell their crap to other "boss babes" on their journeys.

Don't be them. They are repulsive. Educate yourself on what you need to know in your business. If you make yourself an expert in your specialty, then you can say you're good at it.

But without those hours under your belt, you're not really good at it ... yet. I wouldn't call anyone good until they can replicate their results. Don't worry if you can't do this yet. Keep practicing and working, and you'll get there soon enough.

Until you reach that goal, don't even think of stepping into the coaching arena. You need to reach the level where you have enough experience to compare your current results with your past. Then you are ready to coach.

Also, for the love of God, don't be a coach if #fitnessismypassion is your mantra. That is not genuine and not what this book is about.

I'm not saying you can't have a good personal experience. Good for you for losing 40 pounds. Reshaping your body is significant. Nobody is denying that. You get to feel the pride of your accomplishment. But it doesn't make you an expert. It doesn't mean you've taken classes that teach body physiology or that you know how the muscles work, how to move off stubborn plateaus when the weight just won't budge, or that you're aware of how different body types, genetics, injuries, and past histories impact a client's current strategy.

You don't have that knowledge because you haven't sought it out. You randomly got up, worked out, and lost 40 pounds. That worked for you. It doesn't mean it's going to work for everybody else, and it's irresponsible to say that you are now an expert because you've done it for one person—yourself.

If you don't know what you're doing, own up to it. Don't try to play God. It's dangerous. Everyone has just one body. If you break someone's to a point where they can't recover, it screws them for the rest of their life. Even if they can recover, and you don't have the credentials, it's wrong. You are causing them needless pain and stress in their life.

If you learn all about your niche, do the work and build your brand, you *could* become a coach. If you learn to help people solve their pain points, you *could* become a coach. But don't start selling people … yet.

OUR SUPPLEMENT COMPANY

One of my mentors and friends coached me on our supplement company by giving me two phone numbers. Then, he stepped back and made me figure out every other step.

A couple of months later, we were chatting on the phone when he said something I'll never forget: "A good coach will help you every step of the way. A great coach knows the value of learning by figuring it out. They will guide you in a direction."

Funny how guys worth billions know that you only need to be pointed in the right direction and unleashed.

My coach was right. I learned more by implementing suggestions and adjusting my tactics to the results I wanted than having someone apply the recommended steps to fix what didn't go right.

IF THE GREATS STARTED FROM SQUARE ONE AGAIN

If Billy Gene, Andy Frisella, and Ed Mylett had to start over with the same 1,000 followers and $1,000, they would replicate exactly what they have done to get to where they are today.

Billy Gene would restart helping people with their marketing for free, and within a year, he would be the king again.

Andy Frisella wouldn't change a step he has taken to get to where he is today.

The same would be true of Ed and his financial companies. First, they would become the expert, *then* they would charge money.

It's always a good idea to study what the greats do then strategize how you can apply their tactics to your business.

If you're serious, spend the next two years learning. By the way, if you're learning, you don't need a coach!

If I opened a restaurant next to the French Laundry eatery tomorrow, I would fail. Just because I've eaten at a restaurant doesn't mean I know anything about owning or operating one. That would be a completely asinine and reckless thing to try. It would be a complete and total disservice to the customers who wanted a high-caliber dining experience.

This kind of thinking is the same insanity that makes people believe they can just pop up in a coaching business.

Before you take on the title of "expert," understand that when you call yourself one, you're supposed to have experience in the trenches. If a client comes to you and says, "This is not working, and I don't know how to fix it," you are expected to know how to fix whatever is upsetting the customer. It's a reasonable expectation. Don't you have that expectation of everyone you hire? Isn't that one of the big reasons you hired them?

Be a little less green before you start asking for the green.

As the coach, you should have an idea of which direction to recommend. Be well-versed in how you will advise yourself before you start advising others.

WHY YOU'RE BROKE

One of the reasons you're broke is that you're hiring coaches when you're not ready. That's called "doing it wrong." We all want to collapse time and gain 20 years' worth of knowledge today. But there is no substitution for going through learning experiences yourself.

You can't time collapse your learning when you haven't put in any work. You might be able to shortcut some corners, but you can't instantly gain 20 years' worth of knowledge. You don't want to anyway, or you'd only be robbing yourself.

The long road is the shortcut. Full stop.

No coach will build a successful business for you. None of them are so bored running their real-life successes that they want to babysit a wannabe who can't show up every day and at least bang their head against a wall. They want you to care more about your results than they do. And you should.

Oh, and if you're in a rush and hoping a coach will provide a distraction so that you don't have to do the work, don't hire one.

If any of these excuses ring a bell for you, you're not ready for a coach. And unless you do some massive inner work, you won't ever be. Your direction is also, in part, determined by the work you do.

YOU ARE ALL THE THINGS

When you first open your doors, you do all the jobs.

You are the CEO.

You are the founder.

You are the business manager.

You are the marketing manager.

You are the social media content creator.

You are the video editor.

You are accounts receivable and payable.

You are sales.

And you are the janitor.

Then your business gets to a point where it grows so much that you need to allocate some of those roles to others, and you hire people.

When you break free of these roles, your direction becomes clearer.

When it's time to pivot your focus and the jobs you do, at least you will have learned how to do all the roles since you have been responsible for them since you opened your doors.

That comes in handy because you now need to train people to do these tasks. They take jobs off your plate; then you fill your plate up with more until you are overwhelmed again and have to hire once more. It's a cycle of lather, rinse, repeat.

The specific responsibilities of each job are built by doing the job. Then you can push off what you don't need to do anymore. That's the smartest way to empty and fill your plate.

That feeling of overwhelm when you need to shove chores off your plate is a good indicator that you might need a coach. But while hiring a coach is great, hiring a team is even better. When you get to that point, it means you are busy figuring things out and growing by yourself. Take pride in that and move forward.

A coach won't come in and blow up your business or tell you how stupid you are for managing a process the wrong way.

Don't forget, your team will always be a greater asset than any coach. Give them due credit as they are actually doing the work with you. They are growing with you. You are in this with them. The coach provides a 30,000-foot view. They may see a pothole, an incoming mistake, or have relevant advice, but they also don't know the inner workings of your business.

The most important strategy you can apply when working with a coach is knowing when to implement their suggestions and when their advice doesn't apply.

Also, a great coach will never tell you the steps to get something done; they will tell you the *concept* to apply so you can customize it for your business.

Hiring the right team and having the right people in the right places allows you to slowly remove yourself from a position or facet in the company. And I know you're eager, but you can't rush this process. You need to build the job you want your replacement to do and the system you want them to follow WITH the person replacing you. It is important that they help you build it. This ensures buy-in; it makes adjustments and mistakes incredibly easy to handle because of the open line of communication during the development process.

The biggest reason entrepreneurs stall is because they stop filling their plates and start filling morning tee times. I have seen older business owners who are set in their ways take their foot off the gas only to get smashed by the hungry up-and-comers. Don't pawn off your responsibilities prematurely or before your profits say you can.

WHERE DO YOU TURN?

Going through growth is a confusing time. You're taking on all the jobs and seeking mentorship from somebody who's been there before. You might have thoughts like, *Do I hold onto this particular job or let it go? How do I let go of the jobs I need to? How do I hire the people I need to help me? How do I create a job description? How do I scale? Am I making the wrong decision? Do I need a coach?*

**If hiring a coach will create a financial crunch,
how can you better spend your money?**

61

Maybe after questioning everything, you decide you do need a coach. Let's put some more thought into it before you jump into it.

If you know you need to go in a new direction, you might be able to get what you want without a coach. Maybe you can join a Facebook group? Maybe you can become part of a fitness mastermind? Maybe you can listen to a free podcast hosted by the coach you're considering hiring?

Check out the content of the coaches you're considering. Ensure that it makes sense to take their advice. What mistakes have they made? Good podcast hosts and business people will share that with you. They see an opportunity in teaching you all about their missteps.

If you don't want to feel alone, you can also talk to a friend who has a similar business and ask them about the problem you're having and how they would solve it. You do need people in your circle whom you can talk to and bounce ideas off of. That doesn't mean you need to hire them.

CHAPTER 7

BUT I LIKE THEM

"You know you're codependent when you feel guilty for everyone else's mistakes."
—*CodependencyQuiz.com*

Liking a coach is not a strong enough reason to open your wallet and give them a bunch of money. It's kind of like hiring a prostitute—especially if you need to have your brain—or something else—stroked. "Make me feel good, but I'm going to give you a bunch of money to do it."

If you hire a coach to hear how smart and great you are, you're hiring somebody to stroke your ego as you're stroking their ego. If they're a big enough coach, they won't care or even recognize that you're trying to stroke their ego. They might think it's cute that you hang all over them—or they could get intensely annoyed. Don't roll the dice and chance offending them. Either way, when you're new, you won't register as one of the people they entertain and think about on the daily—you know, their co-workers, friends, and family.

Good coaches connect with their clients and provide continual value. They'll work to keep that connection going. They might also have a team of people in all the places they can't be at once. You may not get one-on-one attention, depending on the services you bought. Just make sure you read the agreement well.

While we're at it, let's cut straight to the point. Your connection is not established by simply following someone on social media.

We might feel like we know someone after we stalk their page a little, but it's not true.

Does this sound familiar? *Heyyyyyyy, I saw they went to the beach! Oh man, I like going to the beach, too. Hmmm, that's her favorite sandwich. That's so cool. I love me a good Reuben. Oh, he's been married twice. I've been down that road, too, with my blended family. I bet we would get along great and have a blast hanging out.*

You are salivating over a shiny wrapper. You know nothing of what's underneath that wrapper, and you could be biting into a year old Mounds bar covered in mold. That's what you're doing to yourself every single time you attach to a person that you know nothing about.

Social media is addictive, and that makes it hard for us to detach. But that's another layer of self-awareness. When we spend too much time on these platforms, our perception of other people that we don't know on social media is like having a long-distance relationship and thinking that you know everything about that person.

Of course, you don't. There's lots to be discovered.

You've never shared a bathroom or kitchen with them; you've never split the utility bills between the two of you. You've never observed their sleeping habits. You know more about what you don't know than what you do. Stop fooling yourself and shut your wallet already.

These shiny sham coaches might be great at making you think you know them—but they're either a gifted marketer or someone on their team is.

Differentiation is critically important in your business, so don't just mindlessly follow a huge throng of people to the same coach. Those people are just mesmerized by that shiny wrapper, and their decision to follow that person has nothing to do with that coach's credibility.

Remember, there are more than just a handful of coaches to choose from. Some of the best coaches are less flashy, but they definitely want to focus on you.

IF YOU'RE CODEPENDENT, DON'T HIRE A COACH

This is a very tough subject to bring up, but we need to talk about it. It's similar to what we talked about—needing validation or the company of other people so that you don't feel alone. But you do feel accepted. Codependency is unhealthy; it is a mark of faltering self-esteem. People looking for this type of approval from others don't want to rock the boat. They are too busy trying to be liked. Some call them people pleasers.

But I am not a qualified mental health professional, so I am not going to spend much time here.

Merriam Webster[3] defines codependency as "A psychological condition or a relationship in which a person manifesting low self-esteem and a strong desire for approval has an unhealthy attachment to another often controlling or manipulative person." If you identify

---

[3] "Codependency Definition & Meaning." Merriam-Webster. Merriam-Webster. Accessed January 16, 2022. https://www.merriam-webster.com/dictionary/codependency.

with this, you don't do things for yourself; you do things because you want to hear somebody say, "That was a really good decision," "You're a smart person," "I love what you did with your marketing," and so on.

When you are codependent, you aren't detached enough to make decisions that make sense for you.

I see this in a lot of startups. People start a business with a partner because they don't want to carry the load themselves and want someone in the battle with them.

This is the biggest Catch-22 today's entrepreneurs face. Most great entrepreneurs don't need a partner or didn't start with one.

There are exceptions, but before you decide to engage or partner with someone in business, understand what each of you brings to the table. If those two factors match, BAD IDEA. If your prospective partner does the stuff you hate, AWESOME. Before you agree to any relationship dynamic, get crystal clear on the roles and responsibilities of your partner. How will each person bring equal value to the table?

In franchisees, some guys are pure money players. Some are operators. Some have skills that lend themselves to certain areas like hiring and managing personnel, handling bookkeeping, overseeing systems, implementing culture, etc.

I always stress that anyone considering a partnership answer these questions:

- What are you doing?
- What are they doing?
- What is that worth?

- Who is doing the grunt work?
- Who is doing the marketing?

These are just a few questions to get you started. There are many more you should answer to protect yourself and your partnership.

Iron out these expectations or you will be just another codependent entrepreneur who went into business with emotion, not a solution to a problem. It will get bad fast. I promise.

Will you do your share after you've identified who does what? It's a waste if you don't follow through, whether we are talking about your pending partnership or the long to-do list sitting in front of you. Commit to taking action. If you don't, you are feeding the bad guys in the coaching industry.

People buying services and not doing a damn thing with them is a huge part of why self-development blew up. So don't be a part of the problem.

Shady coaches drool over people who feel unsure about themselves and their businesses. But the irony is these coaches don't even believe in themselves. Now, don't tell me they deserve one red dime of yours! Inept coaches depend on people buying their services and their mile-long line of bull to feel like they are worth anything. They depend on the confusion people feel that comes from not touching their laundry list of chores. The more you leave undone, the more you don't know what to prioritize. A greedy coach sees you coming. You have a problem, and it is easy for them to provide the solution. *You aren't completing your tasks. Simple,* they think. *I'll just tell them to do the work. That's gonna make me look like a genius.*

But once they sign you and you tell them about your real problems, they have no idea how to help you. Their only goal is to money grab as fast as they can—not help you overcome obstacles on the path to your goals.

If you have identified with any of what you read here, let me save you some money, time, and energy. Getting real with yourself is the best thing that you can do right now.

There's no crime in feeling unsure, but if you are reading this and identify with what I am saying, then I encourage you to stop and do some inner work on your core confidence. Until then, don't hire anybody to work with you because it won't be for the right reasons, and you will have a hard time separating from them when it's time to stop working together. Even if you did find success with them, it would be short-lived because you couldn't sustain it—sustainable success requires healthy self-confidence.

One of the best things you can do is fly solo without a coach until you have determined if you need outside validation. Be alone and make decisions without answering to anyone else. Detach and get to work on feeling good about yourself *by yourself.*

People with the strongest core confidence do not care what others are doing. They have learned to operate in their own best interests despite the noise from the peanut gallery.

I recognize that you might choose to be in the company of people who tell you what you want to hear for deep reasons. Maybe for a chunk of your life, you depended on approval from others. Maybe you need to address some familial considerations. Whatever it is, it's okay. And never forget, you can change any time you want to.

Someone else's approval of you doesn't build you up and help your business' longevity. You have to get that from yourself, just like you must get the momentum and thrill of operating your business from yourself.

If you can't separate from the need to hear you're doing okay, you're not okay. You're making decisions based on emotion, and this is very dangerous for your longevity—as in, you won't have any. Business must be run with a steady hand. You need objectivity so you can see clearly what you need to do, not how you *feel* about what you need to do. That doesn't matter.

In fact, many times in business, our feelings can get in the way.

Being honest is the first step to understanding if you are entering into a codependent relationship or a coaching agreement. That's a recurring theme in this book for a reason. You have to know without a doubt what you need so you can find the best solution for yourself.

Ask yourself:

- Am I lonely?

- Am I confused?

- Am I overwhelmed?

- Am I struggling with the decisions I've made?

- What would make me feel better?

- Would I be in this situation and handle it better if there was someone beside me?

If you think you are hungry for the company of another person—that's okay. Realizing these hard truths about ourselves that we may not like is always okay.

That's another theme in this book: Accepting ourselves as we are, including all the decisions we have made that we might disagree with. We have to know what we have done, how we feel about it, and what we need before we can research who to work with and who to vet.

Some ideas for you if you are craving approval and company:

- Do not take destructive action (obviously)
- Join a Facebook group (that has less of a chance to turn your business on its head)
- Join a local chapter of your industry or field
- Make regular appointments to talk with an owner in a similar business
- Focus on the tasks that need to be done
- When you encounter a challenge, consult an industry professional (not necessarily a coach).

If, after answering these questions, you still feel like you need a coach, continue your search for one. But be mindful to take your time learning about the coach, the ROI, and their proof of success.

CHAPTER 8

GOOD MARKETING ISN'T GOOD COACHING

"Some people are real. Some people are good. Some people are fake,
and some people are real good at being fake."
—Unknown

You've ingested a lot of information on what you should and shouldn't do when it comes to vetting a coach. But how do you sift through the information the prospective coach gave you? How will you know you are making a good decision?

In an unfamiliar industry or niche, you must know what to ask for, so get very familiar with the key performance indicators (KPIs) that you can use to gauge a coach's performance.

Since a spammy coach won't tell you the truth you need to know, it's your job to protect yourself and figure out the good measurements to watch for. Uncaring coaches make their living off you not doing your homework, which is another reason you need to care more than them to get at the truth.

KPIs give you data to determine if the coach is getting good results that make sense for your motivations. When I started out, I validated a succession of growth for any prospective coach. I studied the years they had been in business so I could see their volume. For example, I would look at the year 2018, then compare the next year, and so on. Any coach I'm considering better have increased their numbers year over year.

When I looked at Andy Frisella's statistics, I confirmed that he'd grown his companies for well over two decades. As I scrolled through all his social media postings, his progress was right out there in the open. I noted when he opened his first store, when he built his first headquarters, and what he did in the interim before building his second headquarters.

If a coach doesn't have years of social proof behind them, you shouldn't hire them. If you are trying to be a coach and are in the same situation, you shouldn't be a coach in life, fitness, business, or any other area. You're not helping anyone with your lack of experience.

When I examined how Ed Mylett was performing, I could see his succession and track the decisions he'd made to grow through his social media. There it was, everything he had done, all documented.

I also witnessed from both Andy's and Ed's social media posts that sometimes growth was a little stagnant. Their social media account wasn't only full of glossy pictures, photos, and positive events. They were both committed to sharing their truths and not hiding anything from anyone. When I saw that, they instantly earned my respect.

By showing their hands, Andy and Ed built credibility in my mind. With that settled, I started researching the testimonials of past clients and looked at their business reputations. A helpful hint: When you are snooping on a coach, Google their name and add in some keywords like "ripoff reports" and "scam." Then scroll and see what people are saying.

When reading reviews, teach yourself how to read between the lines. Most reviews tell you more about the writer than the person or company in question. If the reviewer is lazy, hasn't done much with their life, or just wanted a friend and got butt hurt, it's pretty obvious from the intent and tone they used.

Also, remember that every opinion is only one side of the story. Take what you read with a grain of salt. Consider what the other side likely is on a review that hits below the belt and is designed to tear a person down—without mentioning a legitimate beef.

On the other hand, if you Google a prospective coach and they come up clean, it's time for more research.

Explore how they're running their business from the inside. Do you know someone who knows them? What can they tell you? Are they cycling through people, or does their staff stick around? Are people happy working there? What's the culture like? What do they stand for? Do you agree with it? Get at the deeper realities of the coach and the people they surround themselves with.

If, as you are Googling a coach, you see impressive marketing, that doesn't tell you anything. They might have clever copy, fantastic graphics, and hit people at the right time of day. You might see a lively Facebook group. All of these are great elements of running a visually appealing coaching business, but that doesn't mean they're going to be a good coach.

Being good at marketing is not the same as being a good coach.

Being a good coach depends on the guidance you provide and the time you take to get to know your clients. Determining what they truly want that's unique to them will help them and benefit their situation. A coach might be skilled in marketing but have no clue how to lead people.

Don't forget that some people hire marketing companies for this exact purpose—to look amazing!

These companies know how to make them look intriguing and compelling, so you want to engage.

They make you laugh.

They're clever.

They're edgy.

That's knowing how to captivate; it's not knowing how to coach.

Slick marketing companies do this on purpose to bait you. Don't fall for it.

CHAPTER 9

HOW TO TELL WHEN A COACH IS FULL OF CRAP

"People who play roles will eventually forget their lines.
Pay attention."
— Unknown

This chapter gives you the goods on discovering who is running the game. I'm also going to dispel some myths that people believe when they sign up for coaching.

Here's how to tell when a coach is full of crap:

1. **How is the coaching business run?**

   Are you hopping on a weekly Zoom call to ask questions? Will the leader of the organization speak on a topic of the week? Will you be expected to interact and ask questions in a Facebook group? Do you understand the rules of the Facebook group and know not to solicit? Do you know if this coach or organization sends out emails? Are you expected to use an app? Will you have to pay for this app? How else can you utilize this app in your life?

   My wife is in a basic level one entrepreneur group. Everyone in the group is expected to work out, take care of their body, do the work to reach their goals, and be a good person. This is a fine group for her to be in. It serves her purpose. But if I wanted to learn email marketing, this would not be the group for me. You should know what the group will give you before joining.

This group is perfect if you want to have a little accountability and make entrepreneur friends.

Another example is John Maxwell. He is a prolific leader. If you are looking to improve your leadership skills, his organization is a good fit. Check around on his website for programs you can join and read about what you will be expected to do. Side note: Don't join on the very day you start your research. Only commit to an organization or coach when you understand what they expect from you.

Don't be dazzled by a famous name before understanding what you will receive in exchange for your payment. Just because you are checking out a well-known name doesn't change the rules of research. No matter who we are talking about, I don't want to guess what a coach wants from me, and I insist on knowing if they are not in alignment with my goals.

Coaches who don't know what they stand for, how they will help you, and have vague information on their websites, are not for you. If you don't understand what they offer, you will have ZERO clue about how to apply it.

2. **Beware of coaches who stalk you.**

Coaches who chase after you for your business are probably not worth your money. Legit businesses will not stalk you because they typically have a team of salespeople who follow up or email automation. The people who are trying to get you to sign up and riding you are desperate for your business. That is a huge warning sign for me, and I hope it will become one for you.

Of course, nothing is absolute, and in some cases, the people trying to reach you can see an advantage to working with you. Maybe they believe you would experience great results. Maybe they want to get closer to you because of what you do or who you know. Don't be in a hurry to decide. ALWAYS do thorough research.

It's more likely that companies and coaches stalking you don't want to lose business and are on the prowl to close a deal. To put it in perspective, if a large organization lost one client, they wouldn't feel too much pain. But an entrepreneur just getting their feet wet would feel the crunch. If they only had three clients, losing one means 33% of their income goes away.

Here's a personal example. By the time this book comes out, I will have sold close to 100 locations. You can imagine at that level the coaches who helped me get there don't have time to spend trying to get people to personally sign up for their courses. Their time is spent growing the business, acquiring different locations, and operating at a 50,000-foot view versus a 5,000-foot view.

As you entertain working with a particular coach, consider their intentions when they ask you to join their masterminds, programs, modules, and courses. Do your research to learn who to avoid.

3. **Does this coach rely too heavily on social media but not really offer anything else?**

Yes, I talked to you about the benefits of joining social media to meet people, expand your network, generate new leads, and create new opportunities. But a coaching organization built heavily on social media throws up red flags. There has to be more below the surface.

I'm hopeful that this chapter provided you with the basis of what you need to know when seeking a coach, learning where to go for resources, and when to say no and walk away. Make it a habit to always do your research to learn what your prospective coach has built that will benefit you. If they haven't built anything so far, cross them off your list.

CHAPTER 10

MEASURING ROI: WHAT ARE YOU BUYING?

"The measure of success is not whether you have a tough problem to deal with, but whether it's the same problem you had last year."
—*John Foster Dulles*

In this chapter, the ROI has to do with you. What kind of stats and improvement can you expect for your business when you hire a coach?

Besides cutting my tax bill, my goal was to find others like me in the fitness industry who had more locations. I specifically wanted to know what they could offer in the way of systems and marketing. I don't mind telling you that the best thing I did for myself at the time was admitting that I couldn't do it alone anymore.

DO THEY ADAPT?

Before we dig in any deeper into the gist of this chapter, measuring ROI and understanding exactly what you're buying and how it will improve your business, I want to share another piece of the coach vetting puzzle.

You need to know and expect that the
coach you'll be working with will adapt.

No one can run a business in the exact same way they've run it for the last 5-10 years.

Part of a coach's job is understanding it's not a stagnant undertaking. Under your job description and roles and responsibilities, write down that you'll be expected to adapt.

You're adapting to technology, trends, emerging information about your prospective clients, and what's new in the industry. Think about: What new needs do your clients have that have not been addressed? As a coach, it is on your shoulders to figure this out. You owe it to your clients to pay attention and give them the best of you and the best in the industry. Obviously, the same logic applies to any coach you're considering hiring.

A coach practicing that level of flexibility means business. They're here to stay. A coach intent on staying has more skin in the game. They want you to have a solid place to receive information, guidance, knowledge, and actionable content you can apply to your business. They're not going to be a fly-by-night operation and expect to last. They will know this. This is a good sign. Select a coach like this.

I'm glad I did because I needed that updated knowledge and commitment to achieve what I have so far. My story would've been different had I chosen a coach who didn't care about my results and phoned it in when it came to their continuing education and dedication.

I remember one of the 10X programs I bought from a "coach" included only an invitation to a Facebook group. There were no emails, background information, personal help, or relevant data as to what they pitched. I left after ten days and chalked it up to being scammed. Thanks, Bert.

A coach who adapts is much more likely to check the boxes on your personal criteria that will allow you to grow. A coach pushing out the same old BS that worked a decade ago will do nothing for you.

ARE THEY SHARING CONCEPTS YOU CAN APPLY?

As I committed to learning, I found answers I didn't even know I needed. Yes, I had an idea of the questions to ask and knew what I should probably do for my business. Still, I committed to learning the answers other people could teach me.

That's when I was introduced to the concept of operating *on* your business, not operating *in* your business.

So many people don't understand that you have to BUILD a business before you can GROW a business. Working ON your business requires profit, systems, a team, and so much more that you can actually grow and scale.

If you're not familiar with this saying, just know that you optimally grow when you work on your business. Don't get distracted by thinking you will grow to a point where you can step out of your position. Get used to working in the dirt and getting the ball rolling before even thinking you deserve that.

This means we're not doing client work yet.... We're working on getting more clients and business branding, for example. We might work on marketing. We might work behind the scenes and re-engineer our processes. We might collect outstanding invoices. Working on the business means doing what we need to do to grow the company. Client work doesn't fall under this umbrella.

Imagine a car mechanic. He only makes money on his clients' cars. The cars are IN his business.

If he hired and managed 12 mechanics, he would have to build support systems so these mechanics could succeed. When he does this, he is working ON his business.

Most people build jobs, not businesses. But you cannot build a salable asset business if you have a key dependency. You must be able to interchange the parts and repeat the performance.

Ego can be a massive problem at this stage, and rightfully so. No one may ever be as good as you at what you do, but understand that if you can get them close and produce 300 of you, your income goes way up, and you have built something other people want to be a part of.

When you are working in the business, you are working within the areas that bring money to your business. You might be doing some client work, whether that's working one-on-one with a client or creating content for them, you're applying yourself in an area that enables your business to make money, but it will not further business growth. You won't be scaling or progressing the business.

Clients are and will always be your most important asset. They are the transactional piece of your business. If you don't stay focused on their experience and ways to provide more and better service, nothing else that we have talked about matters. You will stall your growth and fail.

Always be client-oriented in what you do inside or for your business. Never allow your face-to-face interactions with clients to be watered down or less than your acceptable standard, or you will never be able to work ON your business.

Learning this little trick allowed me to divide up my tasks more cleanly so I could figure out what percentage of time I was spending on each area. Knowing this will also help you make time for working on your business. Sometimes when we are working *in* it, we mistake that for working *on* it. Understanding the difference creates a stronger, more balanced, and profitable business.

MY ROI HAD TO DO WITH ME

When I joined Arete, I was around people in similar situations as me. I was very curious about those several levels above me, as anyone would be, but I was focused on gathering the information to help me solve the challenges I was having I was having in my business at that time. Since I was trying to scale my business, I met people who had multiple locations and could recommend additional tools I could use. I met people who could talk to me about debt leveraging. Eventually, I asked to talk to people who could help me save money on taxes. The network didn't fail me. Multiple people recommended solid experts. That was a measure of ROI for me.

Being involved in this community assisted me in doing what I wanted and taught me the smartest way to do it. I also didn't know who to reach out to prior to Arete because I didn't know who to trust. Being in a group of people I can trust is a huge measurable ROI for me.

MEETING PEOPLE YOU TRUST

When you study luxury marketing, you learn that wealthy people will not Google services. They will not search for roofers in their area, for instance. Instead, they will talk to a trusted source in their life. They'll put the question out to their friends: "Do you have a roofer you trust? Can you introduce me to the person who did the roofing work on your house?" That's just how the elite segment operates.

I wasn't interested in finding another marketing company to take my money and disappear or do a crappy job. I wanted recommendations from someone who had worked with an individual personally and had gotten great results. That's another way to vet someone.

I wanted to be around people who had a stronger skill set than me so I could pick their brains. I did my best to offer as much value to them as I could because I understand it's a two-way street, and I was trying to grow, too. Doing this opened the door to meeting more and more people.

I had tapped into a pocket of quality people who told me all about the true networks and groups making a difference in their lives. Since that day and joining Arete, it's turned up my business. My strategy was borrowing trust until I could build my own.

WHOLE FOODS OR WAL-MART? WHERE DO YOU WANT TO SHOP?

Arete was the experience I was looking for.

Here's a fun fact for you: I would rather shop at Whole Foods than Walmart. Sure, I might pay a little more, but I'm paying for the people I'm shopping with. I'm paying for the experience. I'm paying for better quality food.

I don't want to be around the dude wearing a mesh bag that oranges are sold in—for clothes—his nipples hanging out through the mesh. Walmart pretty much lets everybody in, and there doesn't seem to be any criteria that goes into selecting which foods they will sell. If you can put it in your face and it's edible, they will stock it. That's not what I'm after.

**I want better for myself because I deserve it.
But I also want to support a company that
wants to give that experience to other people.**

In contrast, Applebee's gave away 10x tickets in containers of popcorn. There we go again with the zero barrier to entry and what it can create anywhere—a lower-level environment. That was definitely apparent.

THEY GAVE ME WHAT I NEEDED TO KNOW

I didn't know how to grow quickly—at a pace I desired—without jeopardizing everything I had built. And I wasn't about to hemorrhage a bunch of money without imperative proof of what I would get back. I didn't just leap into joining Arete. I did all the homework I talked to you about in the earlier chapters of this book. I determined that it was a sound investment before they got my hard-earned money and I put anything on the line.

It's scary to scale. So many people are afraid to pull the trigger and bring on someone else. Hiring one person is an exercise in trust. Hiring a marketing company is an ongoing exercise in trust. But you can't stop yourself from stepping forward and bringing people on. You can't be afraid to say you don't know everything. It's one thing to say I don't know everything, so I'm just gonna hire any old guy or gal to help me. It's another to say I don't know how to do this, and I need real help. Then when you *get* the real help, it's yet another exercise in courage to follow through on the steps you've been advised to take to grow your business.

Being around the right people who can offer business and personal support is a great ROI that will pay off indirectly, but still benefits you.

GET SPECIFIC ABOUT YOUR ROI

I can count up my ROIs. You should be able to do this, as well. One of my wins was meeting people who wound up buying my franchise locations. A second was receiving the priceless advice to reformulate our supplements and change our entire business model to get us well on our way to a 9-figure buyout.

What will your ROI be?

If you say, "I want to make back my investment," that's not really an ROI, is it?

Think about it this way: One of the words in ROI is "return." That means you need to earn more than you paid out. Have you thought about how you will make your money back and then some? What are your plans? You must know your goals so you can achieve them.

Do you see why I'm keeping on you about needing to know what your business needs??

In case my words are falling on deaf ears, I will cover all that in the coming chapter. Keep reading!

CHAPTER 11

HAVE A GOAL,
THEN DO SOMETHING WITH IT!

"The only impossible journey is the one you never begin."
—*Tony Robbins*

As I touched on briefly in the Introduction, you should know when you play at being an entrepreneur or influencer, everyone knows.

You're not fooling anyone above your eye level. Even if you're not a fake, you will do damage to your career when you're in the company of scammers.

If you keep acting like an influencer but aren't really one, knowing you won't attract anyone above you, what are the odds that you will elevate or reach your goals?

DON'T BE AN EVENT ENTREPRENEUR

Are you familiar with the type of person I call the "event entrepreneur"? This is a person who makes the rounds of events ad infinitum. They go through the *motions* of taking action but *never* truly do. If you are one of these people, you might feel like this is what you are supposed to do. From the outside looking in, it's what you see everyone else doing.

Let me burst your bubble.

You're watching the wrong people. Besides, if you haven't been working, doesn't that seem odd to you?

Stop signing up with every coaching group or mastermind you can. Strive for some exclusivity in your coaching to build loyalty. If you can relate to "I just went to another event and got #motivated," pay attention before you lose everything.

The people making millions and billions don't waste time playing little games. A respectable business is not a game. Stop treating yours like one.

Coaches make bundles of money—because of event entrepreneurs … like you. Makes you a little sick to think they are only focused on sucking you dry, doesn't it?

Successful entrepreneurs, influencers, and business people don't have the mindset to throng together like a bunch of sheep. They look at what they need to do based on what their business needs.

Sometimes, they might need more information on how to effectively implement social media content that will generate high-value leads. Sometimes, they might need to put their processes under the microscope and learn where they are shortcutting or duplicating work. They might need to learn their methods aren't scalable or sustainable.

You want to attend these events for the betterment of your business. Don't attend them to get drunk in your red bottoms and flaunt your foolishness on IG to make people thirst over you—so you can do nothing for them.

Networking and meeting cool people come from going to these events, but that is not why you go.

It doesn't matter what someone else is doing if it is out of step with what you need. Don't go if it won't benefit you. Don't spend the money you could apply elsewhere to get greater results from. Be secure enough in yourself to go your own way, even if that means you have to travel part of that road alone. You want to be a baller. *That's* being a baller.

Maybe the worst thing about being an event entrepreneur is that when you run this circuit, you will meet the same damn people over and over again.

If you have to join seventeen networks, what's the purpose? Have you taken the time to think about that, or are you determined to hop on every plane you can and snap up any ticket available to look like a big shot? Here's another harsh newsflash: When you do this, no one believes you *are* a big shot, a person worth reckoning. And the people who see you at these similar events all the time will smell the bull.

They see that you have no idea what you're doing, and in some cases, they love it. You make them money, so they'll talk nicely to your face, but the minute your back is turned, they're rolling their eyes.

You are more willing to pay money to them than you are to funnel money into your business in a quieter manner that will pay off. *You are more loyal to them and their growth than you are to yourself.*

Uncomfortable yet?

Good.

> **Growth comes from discomfort.**
> **The best growth comes from choosing discomfort.**

IS YOUR NETWORK REALLY YOUR NET WORTH?

That is a dangerous phrase. It gives people what they think is a goal to shoot for—to get around people worth a lot more than them.

Come on. Don't be dumb. You're better than that and should want more for yourself.

Let me apply a meaningful spin to this saying: "Your network is the *net of your work*. It is the *sum of the work you've done.*"

Think about it this way. Elite and luxury clients will not want to do business with a person who hasn't proven themselves, hasn't tirelessly worked in the industry, and has no strong social proof to show they know what they are talking about.

As an event entrepreneur, you are attempting to build a business on no foundation. You are taking the lazy way. If the tables were turned, would you want to work with someone who has a shallow portfolio of accomplishments but impressive social media? Of course, you wouldn't, and don't lie and say you would.

Find someone who can answer your questions, who has dealt with all kinds of challenges, and can advise you of the best solutions to save you pain.

> **If you are being honest with yourself and acting like an event entrepreneur, then you are becoming the very person you *wouldn't* choose to do business with.**

As an event entrepreneur, you will be busy listening to sales pitches, buying the swag and products that are supposed to motivate you and change your life but won't, and joining MLMs you're convinced will help you but will be useless because you don't know how to interact with your network. You won't get anything done, and you will never have time to implement all the cool and expensive tools and tricks you bought because you haven't made the time to do so. Just like you can't sell all day and never deliver the service or product, you can't continually book your calendar with activities that have nothing to do with your business.

But sit down because it gets worse.

AVOID THE LIST

The coaches you admire talk to each other. You're on an unofficial list of twits who show up, buy stuff, go home, do nothing but play with distracting objects like social media, scrape by to show up again, and lather, rinse, repeat. Your actions aren't impressive or admirable and will get you the wrong kind of attention.

People see you pop back up again and think, *why is he back? What is she doing wrong in her business that she is always on the lookout for solutions?*

The truth is you are looking for the secret, the shortcut, and anything that will make it easy for you to avoid the work. *I promise you, the shortcut is in the work. The shortcut is in the experience.* The reason you think you need to attend 37,676 events is because you don't understand there is no secret.

Real influencers see you as running your business WRONG. No one with any substance in any industry on the planet will want anything from you—except for you to buy their shit. But most importantly, they will not seek you out to work with them. In their mind, you don't have what it takes.

Are you that entrepreneur who bounces around from event to event and startup to startup? Or group to group? Have you kept yourself so "busy" that you never had time to implement even a sliver of what you've learned?

One year you're a marketer, the next a coach, and then *Oh, what the hell? I want to publish books!* Land on something and stick to it long enough to create traction and a solid reputation.

Attending these events will not reveal to you the secret that successful entrepreneurs know because there is no secret—only hard work and being willing to learn and act.

HAVE A REAL BUSINESS

Running a business that gets to the big leagues is ugly. It is grueling. It makes you want to quit. You dream about being free from its chains. There are obviously incredible moments where you might feel like you are flying for a while, but then it's back down to earth to do more work.

Demonstrate to the world, your clients, and your network that you are a person who continually puts in the work, and you will gain respect from the giants of industry. Besides, why the hell would anyone respect someone *refusing* to do what people before you have done?

Do you think with your shallow behavior that these giants look at you and aren't suspicious that you want to use them? This is not the way to become a trusted and valued confidante in their network. The only way to do that is by caring about people and showing how much you can help them first. Think about them and solve their pain. That's Sales 101.

To build loyalty (and only after you have properly vetted a coach), do what they tell you to do in the way they tell you to do it. Just because you are afraid to do the work, don't stop. I'm going to level with you—you need big kahunas to last as a power player. You need to be able to step away from drama, self-limiting beliefs, and you need to be a pro at shutting down self-doubt, so it literally doesn't eat you alive.

That's how good you have to be.

When events happen that take the wind out of your sails, you need to know how to get up and get after it again. And you need to be tireless and passionate about what you do like you have no choice but to keep pounding away—because you don't—not if you're all-in.

Any coach you are working with is going to expect that of you. They are there to help you help yourself get on the map. This is how you earn respect for your commitment to yourself and your goals. Do the work. Complete the level. Move up. Do it again. And again and again, until you want to puke. Then do it some more. Ceaseless execution gets you noticed.

Unending work is also part of the entrepreneur life, so get used to it. If you aren't ready for a literal lifetime of work, impact, and putting out fires 24/7/365 for ten years minimum, you will never get where you want to go. FACT.

In this case, when you are executing a coach's services correctly, it makes sense to spend the money. It makes sense to attend the events—because you're not a poser.

I will never understand people who don't hold themselves accountable for how much they've spent. If I buy a service, you better believe I will see it through. I care where my money goes, and I would never walk away from an investment without a return. But this is what event entrepreneurs do—they throw money at a problem but don't stick around. Then they justify doing it again because they love the high of spending money. That's a good way to run out of cash, clients, and business.

It's a good way to never sustainably build any sort of long-term, generational wealth.

Leveling up means being okay, knowing that you don't know everything—and that you're not supposed to. You are supposed to come to a legitimate coach hungry for knowledge and help. A good coach will listen to you when you say, "I don't know how to fix this problem." They will give you the benefit of their experience to bring you out of your rut.

When I listened and implemented the changes that were necessary, my coaches were ready for me and excited to help me because they knew I had done the work.

I might be in a pretty awesome place now, but I *labored* to get there. And I did something else that made an enormous difference.

That said, I am sadly still at the bottom of the mountain. I only just arrived, so now I have to climb it.

STAY LOYAL

I refused to join other groups besides Arete—although I do network in other groups. Arete is the group that gets my money.

I wanted to get more out of it and wanted people to connect with me. I had a strong compulsion to prove that loyalty and put what I knew to the best use. It's important to me to be known as "the loyal guy."

It means something to the people running the group when you invest all of yourself into what they've created.

This is my value: If someone comes to my door hawking a product, I am not buying it if my friend sells a variation of it.

I wouldn't want someone to act like that with me, so why would I do that to them? You will have multiple offers to join 700 groups; we all do these days. I still don't join them. When you treat yourself exclusively, there is a draw and mystery to you. This is what I have experienced over the last three and half years since I first joined Arete.

HIRE A COACH DOING IT RIGHT

One of my coaches works with the Alabama football team. I didn't sign up to work with him because he hit me up in a direct message (DM). In fact, he never approached me. I sought him out, did my homework, and decided I wanted this dude in my circle so I could work with him.

He wasn't extending himself from a place of desperation. When I read his reviews, people LOVED him. There he was doing the work, putting in the hours, holding his own feet to the fire as he did the same for his clients.

Ryan Stewman, who I mentioned earlier, runs another group, Apex Entourage. He is interested in creating lifelong relationships with people. He didn't just throw up a funnel one day and attract people who didn't to believe in his missions. He genuinely wants to help people succeed by addressing their problems and giving them the tools to reach higher levels. That's commitment. But I vetted him, too, and since I met him in Arete, I knew that he had paid respectable money to join as I had. Joining his network made sense. Our values aligned. He wrote the foreword for my first book.

Are you seeing how this works yet?

I'm not currently in Ryan's group, but I respect him and would gladly join as so many others have and extracted massive value. The same applies to Sean Whalen's group, where my wife is currently a member.

It's cool, affordable, and makes sense for many entrepreneurs and business professionals starting out. Both of these guys have spent real time building real value. I trust them. If I ever leave Arete, their groups would be my next places to settle in and level up. Neither of them is chasing me down to buy their stuff. I respect that.

Any coach I hire needs to fulfill a specific purpose.

When I hired Ben (who wrote the foreword for this book), I wanted to be the best at culture and leadership. I take a lot of pride in those two areas and want to keep growing, so I had to have someone who works with the best: Alabama and Nick Saban.

Ben now works with our leaders to make them better than they were the day before. He gives them the tools to build the culture and leadership we want as he teaches them about the BURN (if you don't get this, listen to his podcast, *The BURN*) inside them and how to apply it in their roles to crush it. In doing so, they can share what they have learned and what needs to be done with the people around them.

As my leaders grew their teams, I had to know how they were doing and what was working. I assessed their ability to run the plays they were told to implement. I examined their commitment to our core values and forecasted what the ROI would be if they all got just 10% better through working with Ben.

Needless to say, it's working. I tested what Ben delivered. Now, he is going to work with ALL of our franchises across the country. No one else can say that. This is massive value for me *and* him.

DON'T GET ATTENTION FOR THE WRONG REASON

Before I finish yelling at all the fakers, let me tell you a story of a guy who asked for it. If he thought he would move ahead by getting any sort of attention (even negative attention), he was wrong. I have one word for you: black-balled.

One day a totally clueless guy, an online coach, a nobody, who had friends very close to Andy Frisella, attacked Andy's 75 Hard program. He made a post bashing it, trying to get his 15 minutes of fame, and wound up severely hurting any chances to connect with Andy or have anything to do with him. Andy was pissed—and rightfully so! This dude will never get up the ladder in Andy's world now, and likely in all the worlds Andy's a part of.

I was curious about this moron, so I went through the comments. People were destroying him. After such a beating, you would think this guy would have learned a lesson. Not so. An hour later, I checked his IG account and found his next post asking for five successful entrepreneurs to DM him so they could work less and make more. Stupid dude, you are the antithesis of what you need to do. That one post rippled out and did major damage to his brand and reputation.

Everyone on that elite level knows each other and talks to each other. Ed Mylett talks to Tony Robbins. Dean Graziani talks to Andy Frisella, etc. They have each other's numbers and follow each other.

That basher will be doomed to live a life trying to convince people to give him money. He will not have any repeat business because of the way he is.

The moral of the story? Don't do that!

TAKE THIS INFORMATION AND GET TO WORK

The information and tools I just shared would have saved me a lot of time and money when I was getting started. I am a big believer in sending the elevator back down, and that's why you're holding this book in your hands or reading it on your screen.

I have been there in the middle of the night, worried about the next step to take. I have been at family celebrations trying to stay in the moment, panicked about what I wanted to get done. I've been burned by people taking my money when I didn't know what to look for in a coach, in marketing, or in a business advisor.

There's a better way to vet a coach than rolling the dice and hoping for the best. I wish I had figured that out sooner. Your journey to discovering who is right for you can be shorter and less painful … if you listen to me and take action on what you're reading here.

I want that for you. You want that for yourself. You know what to do. Stop being an event entrepreneur, and turn the page.

CHAPTER 12

YOU DON'T START
AT THE HIGHEST LEVEL

"Don't try to go right to the top in one leap.
Every time you accomplish a goal, you develop the
strength and wisdom to accomplish the next one."
—Chuck Norris

When I started in Arete, the application process was INSANE. Out of 10,000 applications, only 60 people were accepted.

Arete (at the time) was not the best place for a beginner to start. It also had a 5-plus-figure price tag. So, do your research and if you find you're not ready to make that jump—don't!

As we discussed, in that situation, you wouldn't have a lot in common due to the large disparity in experience. What would you even talk about as a newbie meeting with established business people?

Let's imagine the conversation:

Newb: "Hi, my name's Joe Blow, and I started the Go Blow Yourself bubble-blowing business. Man, it's hard finding the right distributor. You feel me?"

Pro: "Hi, good to meet you. I'm Steve Successman. I own 50 different franchises and co-founded an international company, Successman Speed Traps. Maybe you've heard of it? I can't really relate to your situation. Been using the same distributors for five years now."

Newb: "Of course, but searching for the best CRMs, such a problem, right?"

Pro: "We nailed that down in year two. Been running smoothly ever since."

Newb: "I feel that. It's just everything, you know? Trying to figure out who is supposed to do what. I can't keep people on the payroll."

Pro: "Identifying standard operating procedures was done on like day two." *Chuckles. "But hey, bud, good talking to ya."

Newb: "You, too. I'm sure we'll run into each other again."

Pro: "Uh-huh."

What was missing?

Those two people had zero connection, and there was nothing for them to spend any amount of time talking about.

Awkward.

This conversation would never work, and both people would get nothing out of it. It's one-sided. The newb doesn't need high-end coaching on minor details, and Successman has different needs and requires other skills and experiences. Remember our age analogy, that the five-year-old and the 25-year-old wouldn't just chill together? They don't have anything in common. The same is true in this example.

So, what's the best thing to do here?

Avoid the whole experience.

Successman is probably already off on his next venture. He's focusing on an upward trajectory, and now his growth is coming in leaps and bounds. When he levels up, he brings the previous levels, more volume, and money with him. There's more to manage and plan.

Joe Blow, however, will likely muck around in the lower levels of business for a while. If he doesn't devise a plan to pull himself up by his bootstraps, he might never level up. He isn't firmly rooted in his business. There's a lot at stake.

Successman has different considerations. If he loses a client, he probably has 200 others, so he won't be out of business.

Joe Blow prays to hold onto the clients he has, and if even one of them goes away, it will affect a considerable percentage of his business.

But let's backtrack for a minute.

How dumb is it that Joe Blow blew money on attending a high-level event where he might learn some tips that will help as he moves to higher levels later, but they won't do a damn thing for him now?

He could have allocated money for marketing and advertising to allow entrance into a smaller mastermind where he could meet other people who could actually help him. Or he could have invested in new software that would help him balance his business better. I could keep going, but I'm sure you can envision many more intelligent decisions.

VALUABLE PERSPECTIVE

On the other hand, if you spend big money to go to an event to learn practical knowledge that you can apply to your business in real-time, you definitely will see your business differently. You can make decisions about it with no emotional attachment, and you'll have the perspective to view what it truly needs.

Your perspective also tells you that you have to pay to play.

If you want to be in the right rooms, you have to pay to be there. If everyone else has to pay their dues, why would you think you can just skate on in and get the same advantages they have?

It's unfair to those people who have bled, sweated, and cried over what they've built. They forced themselves to stay the course when they wanted to quit, too. Who sacrificed time with their families and refused to spend money on frivolous stuff even though they wanted to just like you.

Running a successful business is a balance between loving what you have created and being protective and making the best choices to further your success.

**Seeing the truth requires maturity and self-control.
You won't get anywhere without these two qualities.**

Remember that before you whip out your credit card. You're going to these events for different reasons than those a little further down the road than you.

You'll get there, but try not to be in a hurry. Be in the place where you are now and learn as much as possible. Seek out the opportunities that fit your current state. Squeeze the blood out of that potential, *then* look for the next reasonable investment in your business.

This is why I recommend you research the type of return you can expect from a coach, mastermind, or event. Don't inflate the numbers; don't run from reality. If all the people you want to hang with are going to an event and you run the numbers, and it's a no-go, stop. You're an adult. You can accept that you should stay home, and you can control yourself from making a destructive choice.

Turn your energy toward finding coaches and opportunities that will help you. Then meet people who are where you are or a level above. As you do this, you will even meet people who are a level below you who you can help.

No one cares if you get the pic with the leader, billionaire, president, concert celebrity, or anyone else—only you. What you really want is the next step. The progress you can see, measure and quantify. The progress you can actually plan for. You can implement real tactics for the level you are on.

Nothing else matters. Every step must be built then taken. That's how anyone who has lasted long enough to succeed plays the game. They've built up a solid foundation every single day. Their stairs led to a destination; they mapped it out and built the path.

The most important people at every event are those on your level or within two levels either above or below. Put yourself in that place, then contribute to the value exchange equally and where you can help people.

Mostly…

Be a sponge.

Read more books.

Save your money.

Act.

THEN you can re-read this book to
get a completely different lesson from it.

CHAPTER 13

VET YOUR NETWORK LIKE
YOU VET YOUR COACHES

"The time to build a network is always before you need one."
—Douglas Conant

In this last chapter, I am flipping the script. Everything you have just read about to help you vet a coach, you can now apply to vet the people in your network.

But before you reach out, stop and think about what you are giving away when you offer up another spot in your network. You're going to be interacting with this person and spending time on them—which translates to spending money on them. Put that way, it might make you a little more cautious. Time is more valuable than money. Always has been. Always will be.

Try to spend time with people who share similar viewpoints. I'm not saying avoid people who have differing opinions (unless they're idiots), but you'll get more out of your time when you spend it with people who want to collaborate with their own lofty visions.

The workaholics all want to band together.

The people making the excuses love to validate their lazy behavior.

When you are with ballers and are ballin' yourself, you lift each other up. You become part of the catalyst in your network's lives.

Just as you want to start on the right level with the right coach, you will do the same with networking. Wherever you are, that's your wheelhouse.

I've now built my business to a level where I am qualified to tell you the truth. So save yourself from the sting of rejection and don't pursue people who won't be aware of you—those big mastermind speakers and leaders who have staff to handle everything.

Remember, the goal of this book is to save you invaluable amounts of time and money. It is about self-assessment, vetting who and what to work with in personal development, then making sure you are measuring the ROI.

Successful networks are built on relationships, so make sure you put in the time to develop them.

People can see a sham a mile away. You need to care about the other person, learn about their life, their kids, what they like to do, and who's important to them.

It's a friendship with business benefits.

You'll be seen as a user and uncaring if you don't show interest in what's going on in the lives of those in your network. If you were receiving that kind of treatment, you would not want to cultivate a relationship with the person treating you that way. Well, it will happen to you if you're not engaging or are engaging for the wrong reasons.

Be a REAL person and a REAL friend. Care about them, not for gain, but for the purpose of caring. Takers don't win; you must be a giver to get positive karma.

When you start building your network, don't make it any harder than it has to be. Just do good and great things for people because you are genuine. You will always get it back. Even if you don't think so, it will be returned. I have never met a genuine, real, caring human who has ever lost long-term. Ever.

ANYONE CAN BE YOUR GOLDEN GOOSE

Treat your networking very carefully. Don't approach a potential person with judgment. You never know who is going to be your golden goose or who might change your life. I met the person who changed my life when I was bartending. She was a client of mine, and I told her that I had a dream of opening my own gym.

This woman had developed trust through working with me, and she and her husband wanted to help by giving me $70,000. As she handed me the check that would change my life and said, "This is to get started," I took it with tears in my eyes and incredible gratitude.

Most people you see walking around you who have real power and influence don't flaunt it. They wear regular clothes, and nothing will signal to you that they might be influential. A person who knows the real value of money won't spend it on stupid crap anyway. If you saw the woman who handed me the check, you would think that she looked like a normal person. So don't assume. If I had done that, who knows where I would be today?

The most important relationships I have built over the years are the ones I entered into with a shared passion. This is also how I built my business to the point where it is today.

At one stage of our business, we had 900 people working with two trainers, but that number didn't matter. We answered their DMs, knew when their kid had a soccer game and what they were up to in their business—all because we cared enough to find out. We all shared that passion for serving people.

Every single one of those relationships turned into another client, which pushed us to open four gyms in four years. So, don't ever forget, you don't know who will change your life.

I might even be the one to do it.

Good people want you to succeed, and entrepreneurs usually want to help you. Most of the entrepreneurs I know love advising others. They get excited about helping people avoid an issue that hurt them and divulging real-life methods that have impacted them for the better.

Your relationships won't be a two-way street all the time. Just do what you can to ensure you are providing value, but also accept that sometimes you will be the person who learns the most. Even out the score then and help someone who can grow from your experience.

Maybe you are not in a position to help anyone right now because you are just starting out. That's okay. As you continue to grow, you will have more resources to offer. After a few years, you might want to invest in a deal with a particular person, or they might want to purchase a product that would help them. Remember what happened when I was introduced to certain people in Arete; it resulted in me being able to sell over 100 franchises in a year.

WHAT DOES IT MEAN TO PAY A COACH?

The last nugget I want to leave you with is that people underestimate the value of someone paying them. It's actually a big deal. When others give you money, they are saying, "I trust you."

Now, a word of warning before you put this book down and run off in search of people to fill your network....

Don't be obnoxious and try and attract people to you in the wrong way. Don't break the rules in groups you are privileged to belong to.

I wrote this book so that you don't get burned.

But I also understand that getting the right coaching and challenging yourself in personal development in today's society gives you a huge advantage. When used properly, it can exponentially help you.

Before you get started hiring anyone, you need to understand how to navigate and vet people to make sure you don't get burned. That's why I've pulled back the curtain and showed you how not to waste money and time when you're hiring people to help you and your business.

If you want to invest in growing your business and brand and if you want to network and enjoy everything the personal development industry can encompass, but you don't know the facts, you're going to get burned.

So many great coaches can truly help you get the results you're after, but you have to do the work to get to where you want to go in your life—this is work you need to do before you pick a coach.

As you evolve on your journey, you should be able to go back and re-read this book and find that everything we've talked about will still hold true.

Personal Development can be a scary adventure, so use the tips I've shared with you in this book to avoid getting burned.

ABOUT THE AUTHOR

Aaron Nash is the Owner of P-Fit the Platinum Standard of Fitness ™, WAYT Nutrition, and the Co-founder of Kids Lives Matter to end human trafficking in the US. He is a husband father, and friend. He started his business in 2016 with only four people in his network after driving 1,300-plus miles across the country to start his first gym after over a decade in fitness.

Since building his companies, he's won several awards and records. None of that matters as it pertains to this book.

He hopes in a couple of years that by following his own advice in this book, he will continue to grow into a household brand that truly enables and empowers people to be healthier, better members of our country.

Don't forget to access your self-assessment coaching form on my Instagram @aaronnash20.

DISCLAIMER

This book is a truthful recollection of actual events in the author's life. The events, places, and conversations in this book have been recreated from memory. The names and details of some individuals or entities have been changed to respect their privacy.

The information provided within this book is for general informational, educational and entertainment purposes only. The author and publisher are not offering such information as business, investment or legal advice or any other kind of professional advice, and the advice and ideas contained herein may not be suitable for your situation.

Any use of the information provided within this book is at your own risk, and it is provided without any express or implied warranties or guarantees on the part of the author or publisher.

No warranty may be created or extended by sales representatives or written sales materials. You should seek the services of a competent professional before beginning any business endeavor or investment. Neither the author nor the publisher shall be held liable or responsible to any person or entity with respect to any financial, commercial or other loss or damages (including but not limited to special, incidental or consequential damages) caused, or alleged to have been caused, directly or indirectly, by the use of any of the information contained herein.